I0441011

Acknowledgements

I want to thank all of those people who have helped me put this book together: Emily Lambert from Forbes magazine for her hours of editing, Emily Younker always encouraging me to keep trying and always believing in me, Ria Mendoza from OrangeJar.com who created the amazing cover and finally my amazing wife April who has always read the first drafts and still tells me I'm a great writer.

Table of Contents

Introduction

Think of your favorite character, the one that changed your life and made you look at people and the world differently. What did the author do in order to bring that character to life? Most likely the author used a combination of techniques in order to make that particular character seem real. Creating this character took many hours of thought and effort -- and probably a few sleepless nights, as the author dreamed of and wrestled with the character's personality and evolution throughout the book.

Sméagol is one of my favorite characters because I empathize with his plight. In order to get a reader to empathize with a creature such as Sméagol, Tolkien needed to create a character that had characteristics shared by everyday people. Tolkien did this by allowing Sméagol to change and struggle, in his case with an outside force that entered his life in the form of a ring. As Tolkien showed the reader Sméagol's struggles, we saw – and continue to see -- that Smeagle was not evil, just couldn't overcome the evil around him. Smeagle's character also provided insights into Frodo's behavior when he tried to overcome the ring and when he failed to follow through in the end. Tolkien truly mastered the art of character development.

Creating believable characters requires that writers master the principles of human behavior. We accomplish this by understanding how people react, change, and make decisions. In essence, we must learn to diagnose our characters just as psychologists diagnose people.

This book combines two passions of mine: writing and psychology. I've studied psychology over the past six years, both through formal education and experience in the field. This has helped me to better understand the human condition. I've worked with disorders in every age group, ranging from complex cases such as schizophrenia and depression to more mild disorders, such as feeling unfulfilled in the office. Working with individuals to change their destructive beliefs and behaviors gives me glimpses into their motivations and thinking. Studying, observing, and ultimately helping people has helped me better understand the ins and outs of individuals and social environments.

These real life experiences, plus years of schooling, have helped inform my writing, especially by helping me create unique and genuine characters. In this book, I share both the knowledge (e.g. psychological studies, terms, and explanations) and valuable exercises (e.g. people watching, observing our own senses, and functional assessments) that can help create complicated and authentic characters that can withstand the scrutiny of readers and critics alike. Readers should empathize with characters. And whether they hate or love those characters, readers should become engrossed in those characters' stories.

Of course, if we as writers spent all our time trying to understand the characters we write about, we would never write. Not all characters require in-depth study. If a character only appears in a book for a few sentences, we don't need to know everything he would ever think or do, only what is important to drive the story forward. On the other hand, we need to understand our main characters well enough to understand their motives, beliefs, and weaknesses. And we can use many aspects of psychology to make characters believable and enjoyable to follow.

When looking at what makes up a person, the who, what, where, and when of a person -- i.e. his or her psychology -- we quickly discover that easy answers are hard to find. Exploring this idea of psychology on my own for a couple of weeks, I came up with a list: spirituality, physical, IQ, mind, core beliefs/schemas, behavior, emotions, conditioning, personality, and psychopathologies. Later I asked a colleague about her thoughts on psychology and got a blank stare. When I gave her a few prompts she contributed several possibilities: beliefs, environment, history, family, culture, thoughts, actions, awareness, and energy. I was struck by her inclusion of energy. She explained her interpretation of energy as how a person connects to the rest of the world, including the people nearby.

You can imagine why it takes years of studying to answer the question of psychology. I won't delve into every aspect of psychology, but I'll provide an overview of theories and studies most pertinent in creating a credible character with the depth needed to capture your audience. I've arranged this book in six chapters that are arranged around different concepts of psychology. Each concept includes aspects that make up a person or character. Also, each chapter contains exercises to review and enhance what we learn from psychology, giving us experiences that will develop our understanding of how people work and behave. Such experiences, in turn, give us the tools needed to create believable characters. At the end of each chapter, we will develop a sample character using what was learned in the chapter. By the end, you should have a complete, sample character formed using the tools, knowledge, and experience gained from the book.

Chapter 1
Physical Characteristics and Functional Analysis

Characterization creates a fictitious character portrayed as if in reality. Interestingly, one reason characterization emerged in 19th century literature was due to the rise of studies in psychology. This makes sense considering psychology studies the human mind and behavior - as well as the study of animal behavior- so why wouldn't it influence how we develop and create our characters? For us to then make believable and complicated characters we need to understand the basics of psychology.

Two ways exist in which a character can be brought to life on the written page: the direct and indirect method. In the direct method the author tells the audience exactly who and what the character is. *The man named Phil was exactly five foot three with dusty blonde hair and a big round nose.* The indirect method shows the audience the character through thoughts and actions of the character and through the reactions of supporting characters. *That must be Phil, Sandra thought as she walked up to him. Even with her short stature, she stood a head taller than him. His nose protruded from his face like a tangerine, making it hard to ignore.* Today, more than ever, we present our characters in a more indirect method; we show our audience the characters rather than telling the reader about them.

A well-developed character in our stories not only keeps the audience's attention, but an agent's attention. Agents look for good characterization, and they expect to see characters developing throughout the story.

Physical Characteristics

When we introduce a character we give a little at a time; we don't bog down the story with extraneous details.

Introduce what we'd notice first about a person: hair, skin, weight, height, etc. Note that when we see a person we generally don't say, oh they are 6'2" and weigh 210 lbs. Our brain automatically registers something about an individual when we first see them, for example, he must have played basketball in high school or wow she needs a vegetable or two. This paints a better picture without giving numbers. Also, we often point out a character's eyes in the beginning, but think back to the eye color of the last person we met. We usually don't remember. Later on, if the character evolves into a key player in the story, then we can introduce the eye color somehow if the detail proves important to the character and the scene. However, as authors, we need to know these details about our characters. We may never write them in our stories, but we need to know them so we can portray them to our reader.

I have a game that has a portrait builder in it which allows me to design how my characters look. I use this to print out a picture of my main characters so that I have a visual of them. I have also heard of other writers picking pictures from the internet and printing them out. This helps us keep our character's unique physical qualities in mind. Most important do they have scars or deformities or oddities. What makes our main character stand out from the crowd? Does the main character have a lightning bolt scar on their forehead? Does the character have a limp? Walk with a shuffle? Or is the story more about the main character not standing out?

This leads us to gender. Prior to the sixties, people perceived individuals as either male or female, black and white. Masculinity and Femininity sat on opposite ends of the spectrum. A healthy man would want to appear as far to the masculine side as possible, while a woman should rate as far on the feminine side as possible.

In 1973 Anne Constantinople claimed that masculinity and femininity reside instead on two separate scales: low or high. A man could fall high on the masculinity scale exhibiting things such as hunting, playing sports, and working on cars and at the same time rating high on the feminine scale by exhibiting feminine characteristics such as cooking, coddling babies, and designing clothes.

Do our characters exhibit society's expectations of how they should act, or do they rebel? Do we put our characters into roles that society expects them to play or are we breaking society norms?

In a novel I wrote, society has expectations for males and females and when they break those expectations they receive a punishment. In our own world, what expectations do we have of different genders and what happens when they go against those norms? This needs to also happen with our characters when they break their society's gender expectations.

How do our characters internalize those expectations? How does going against the expectations of society affect our characters? How do they view others who rebel against society's norms and expectations? How do they cope with such pressures?

When developing the physical characteristics of our characters, keep in mind that as humans we have the ability to empathize with all species. However, the further we get away from species that look like and act like us the less empathy we feel. We need to build on this empathy and recognize that few readers fall in love with a main character that looks like a cockroach; I can smash a cockroach without thinking twice. However, I don't think I could smash a bunny. Due to this human trait many of our Hollywood stars are young and beautiful. Having said this, an important note must be made. Even though readers identify more with characters that look more human we as writers go beyond the "cuteness" factor. We can also help our readers identify with other human characteristics such as love, decency, emotions, friendships etc. In this case a reader can and will fall in love with a cockroach and no longer smash them.

A writer needs to gain the audiences' sympathy for the main character or the book will struggle. The main character must appear similar to the reader in not only physical characteristics but, also psychological characteristics. A good example includes *Watership Down*, even though the characters in the book did not look human, in fact they are rabbits, they had human characteristics and we could identify with them.

An example of this empathy is seen in animal research. When hearing about research conducted on animals we don't want the research to happen even though it helps us out (i.e. medical advancements, consumer products, etc.). We identify with animals because of our fear and empathy. We can picture ourselves, our parents, and our kids in a similar situation. Alien movies scare us because we see ourselves conducting experiments on animals (intelligences lesser than our own) so the possibility exists that an alien life form exists out there, more intelligent than us, could experiment on us as well.

Functional Analysis

In creating our characters, we as writers need to go beyond the outer appearances of our characters. We need to delve into their inner workings and find out their deepest secrets; why they behave the way they do. Functional analysis goes beyond topographical views of objects around us. Topographic view sees things as everyone sees. For example, look around your room and describe what you see. If a friend came into your room they could describe the same things you did. Now imagine you have a clear container of liquid sitting on the edge of your desk that you just drank from. You know what liquid the container holds, but the friend that just came in doesn't. Our readers have this same topographical viewpoint and they may not know more than that. We as writers may know what our characters think and feel, but readers probably don't. Readers will make assumptions, get confused, and ditch the story in frustration if we don't show more than the topographical view.

When doing a functional assessment you must take into account everything that may cause a behavior. What causes the character to blow his nose? Is he allergic to something? Does he have a cold? Or has he just bumped it?

Functional analysis ranges from describing the environment to manipulating the environment to see how different people and things react in the given situation. As writers, we should purposely change certain details in the setting to observe how a character responds to the changes and to explore what it takes for that character to react in a certain way.

When creating a believable character we need to go beyond what they look like and how they think to the point where we understand how they react in certain situations. Here are four things to know about human behaviors: they are understandable and predictable if we have all the information, they are malleable and can be shaped, they occur within a context and not a vacuum, they are learned and can be manipulated. We can understand our characters with these four principles – who they are, how they react, and how they'll change. We can create characters our readers can believe as real.

In order to do this we must become masters of human behavior. We need to know how people behave, how they change, and why they change. At this point we need to plan time when we can do some people watching.

People Watching

An exercise I do often is pay attention to the people around me. As I do this I think about their thoughts. What's on their mind? Are they happy? Are they sad? Are they anxious or depressed? Do they have a new boy/girlfriend? What goes on behind the faces? Take the time to enjoy watching how they walk, how they look, and how they talk on their phones. Talking on the phone is particularly interesting because of how they change when they hang up. The same thing happens when they are walking with someone who then goes in another direction. Start watching people, their behavior and body language can tell you so much about them.

As you watch people keep in mind the seven universally recognized emotions shown through facial expressions: fear, anger, surprise, contempt, disgust, happiness, and sadness. Regardless of culture, these expressions are the same. Communication largely takes place in our facial expressions and mainly in our eyes. We, as writers, need to show our character's emotions by facial expressions. In order to do this, we need to notice facial expressions. Each time you people watch, take a journal and write about the facial expressions you see.

You'll be amazed.

Why Do We Care About People Watching

It's amazing the number of people in this world and yet we never find two exactly alike. I look at my sisters, identical twins, and see how different they are. People ask how I tell them apart, and I reply how can't you tell them apart. They move different. They act different. They sound different. Even though they are identical twins, they are still different.

Our characters must be unique. They must feel different to the reader. This can be done in a variety of ways: how they talk, mannerisms they have, how they look, and how they act in certain situations. Get inside their heads, know them inside and out, so when we put them down on paper they're still alive. We must ensure that they stay multidimensional.

In psychology, when I see a person for the first time, I always start with an intake. I find out about the person, their medical history, family history, and mental illness history – anything that has to do with the person. Were they pre-mature? How was the pregnancy? Was the mother on drugs? The list goes on. We need to setup an intake session with our characters to find out their inner workings and then write down our findings. What are their strengths and weaknesses? Can we diagnose them with any personality disorders or mental illness?

Antagonists

Don't forget our antagonists. This is the person who makes the hair on the back of your neck stand up. When one of my supervisors gets around people who are bi polar, his heart speeds up. Another professor feels unpleasant when she gets around anti-social personalities. It doesn't always have to be extreme, but when a person acts like someone we have had a bad experience with, we automatically recoil. This makes a good villain –the character that makes us feel like we've been to a used car dealer and we know we're getting ripped off. These feelings come from past experiences we've had with certain types of people whose simple body movements or words are just a bit off. We feel something amiss but can't quite tell what it is.

The challenge is to get the reader to feel this way even though they can't see the person. We need to produce characters that readers can see, touch, smell, feel, and remember. We need to make characters with glitches and loose wires consistent to their nature. The subconscious makes the reader uneasy, hitting him/her at the core. This can only be done when we see inside the head of our antagonists.

Exercise: Go to a crowded mall, supermarket or event and spend an hour just people watching. Take a notebook and write about what you see.

Sample characters

In this first chapter we have learned a little bit about functional analysis and how people will never be the same, not even identical twins. In order to create a believable character we can't just copy other characters from literature or even from our own stories. However, in the beginning you will need to draw upon similarities of characters to get started. Think of all the clay pots out there. All potters start with the same form and slowly meld their own original pot out of similar material. As writers we must do the same thing.

As explained earlier we must get deeper into the minds of our characters and diagnose their personalities and traits. We must go beyond just what they look like. We're not ready to do that yet, so we will start with the basics.

Character 1: Sarah literally means princess. In my current work in progress my heroine will need to develop into a leader making Sarah a great name. She has black hair from her mother that has a tint of red when the sun hits it just right. The red tints will help this character stand out.

Her blue eyes come from her father and she is the oldest of four children. Her walk is light and she always has a smile on her face. She is petite at five foot 4 and weighing around 120 pounds. Her complexion is light. Her wardrobe mainly comprises dresses, blouses, and skirts.

Character 2: Ghiyath stands 5 foot 10 and weighs 350 pounds. When writing this character I will use his weight as an identifying physical trait. Hair color black and eye color brown with a pasty white complexion. He wears a red robe that flows around his body and pools at the ground.

Remember, our characters don't have much to them at this point; we are only seeing the topographical view of the characters. A reader wouldn't be real excited with the depth of our characters at this point.

Chapter 2
Talents, Body Language, and Formation of Personality

Talents

Talent, as defined by Merriam-Webster Collegiate dictionary, is a special natural ability or aptitude. Our talents bring us the most joy in life and a feeling of fulfillment. We all have talents; some more than others, but we all have talents.

Our characters also exhibit talents that define them. However, our characters' talents only become beneficial after many hours of practice. We see the big things they practice like magic or sword play, but what about smaller talents like carving or whistling. Our characters deserve more depth, like what do they do as they sit around the campfire or walk through the forest?

What little talents do our characters nurture? How did they discover them? How do we show the reader their talents? Talents, though innate, must have opportunities for manifestation.

As an exercise make a list of talents that you can draw from when creating your characters. This list will grow as you write. Each time you create a new talent that does not exist in our world, such as dragon riding, add it to your list.

Nature vs. Nurture

A person may have talents, but without the right circumstances, those abilities may not manifest. Take Tiger Woods, for example, a great golfer with an innate ability to golf, but what if he had been born in Siberia? How much golfing would he have done in the Siberian cold?

What drives a person's abilities: personality, behavior, etc.? Does nature or does nurture cause this drive? A question debated for years. Both influence who a person is. Like Tiger Woods, a person needs both the innate ability and the opportunity to manifest said ability.

In one of my stories, a woman warrior gets sheltered because of her family's position and she receives no formal combat training. She gets captured, fights in gladiator pits, and survives. She has the talent from birth, but I also created a window for manifestation. I gave her a childhood friend with whom she could duel and practice her innate skill of swordplay. Now she has opportunity to learn and increase her natural abilities to help her succeed.

Personality identifies a person with unique characteristics and exemplifies two sides of the argument between nature versus nurture. These characteristics influence cognitive capacities, motivations, and behaviors of a person in various situations. Where do our personalities come from? Do they change over time? Can we influence the personalities of others? We must not only understand natural born abilities of our characters, but also place them in circumstances where those talents strengthen and improve. Several other debates and assessments on personality exist. These theories derive from theorist's differing philosophical standpoints.

Four other debates concerning the formation of personality are as follows:

Freedom vs. Determinism: Do we have control over our behavior? Are our actions uncontrolled reactions to circumstances, or do we control our behavior and understand the motives?

Uniqueness vs. Universality: Are people unique or do we all have the same nature? Current research leans toward more of the middle ground; we are unique but have common traits. As the father of four children, I side with this contemporary research.

Active vs. Reactive: Do we act through our own initiative or do we just react to stimuli? A majority of researchers tend to take the middle ground, but more and more researchers tend to lean more toward active participants rather than inactive. Rene Descartes said, "I think therefore I am." If I can think about thinking and think about things around me and then act, this is active participation in my actions.

Optimistic vs. Pessimistic: The optimistic point of view believes that we can change who and what we are. The pessimistic point of view believes we can't.

Think about these different categories when creating our characters and how we can develop them in realistic terms. We can develop accurate ways in helping our characters grow through the story. Put our characters in real, change-promoting situations to help develop their talents.

Exercise: Take a moment to create a characters using the two different theories. How did this alter the personality of the characters?

Gestalt Theory on Body Language

Gestalt theory, developed by a German psychiatrist named Fritz Pearls, centers on taking responsibility through awareness of the here and now. Individuals using this theory ask why they feel or act in certain ways now compared to past experiences. For example, people, abused as children, focus on how they feel when discussing the abuse, rather than the feeling of being abused. A Gestaltian therapist makes the clients aware of their physical movements and actions by pointing out things like: "What are you doing with your leg" or "I see your eyes are starting to tear up." By doing this, the therapist identifies differences in how a person acts and what that person says. We/our characters say one thing and mean another. For example, a character may smile while talking about her grandmother dying. A character may appear calm through their voice and words, but they may tap their finger or foot constantly. So, when creating our characters, remember that their actions, their body language may not always match what they say or feel. Body language doesn't lie even if our words do.

By using body language, we hint to readers about the unreliability of our character's actions, beliefs or attitudes, hence the unreliable narrator. This tool allows the reader to actively participate in a story. It builds the tension that keeps the reader reading.

Gestalt theory uses body language in order to better understand people. As authors, we need to understand how to use body language to show our readers what our characters think without telling them, show don't tell. We can portray any and all emotions and thoughts to our readers through a character's body language. Think how we interpret others' body language without trying to do so. Our characters should do this too.

Exercise: Write a short story with no dialogue, only body language; see how much you can tell the reader.

Sample Characters

The table below summarizes a few of the talents that each character has and how those talents developed further. This table will grow as we write our stories. By looking at how the talent developed we can gain greater insight into our characters and their past. For example, below you will notice one of Ghiyath's talents includes punctuality, which developed from the demands of his parents. This lets us know that his parents were strict, perhaps too strict.

Sarah's Talents:

Talent	How Further Developed
Water Controlling	Trained by mother
Swordswoman	Duels with friend
Strong Willed	Taught by parents to be independent
Desert Survivalist	Raised in the desert
Singer	Sang in choir as a child

Ghiyath's Talents:

Talent	How Further Developed
Punctual	Parents demanded punctuality
Memory of People	When meeting a person he makes a point of saying the name several times.
Smooth Speaker	Raised in the political arena
Folds Origami	Self-taught at a young age

Chapter 3
Psychodynamic Theory

Let's explore the basics of different theories to help us develop functional, unique characters to inhabit a story's plot. The first group of ideas comes from Freud's psychodynamic theory. This includes concepts of the id, ego, and super-ego – along with unconscious mind and defense mechanisms.

Id, Super-Ego, and Ego

The id makes up the inner child of a person, the part which desires to feel good and acts on the pleasure principle. The id begins at birth and becomes the disorganized part of us.

The super-ego forms the structured, rule-following part of us. The perfectionist inside of us. Our conscious, representing: our parents, teachers, religious leaders etc.

The super-ego and id perpetually fight with each other – a battle that rages within us. This battle causes the ego to develop within us. Otherwise, nothing would get done.

The ego acts according to the reality principle it consoles the id while being rational. At times, the ego must mask reality and keep the Id in the dark to maintain peace; hence, the unconscious, which we'll discuss later. The ego plays a balancing act, allowing the id pleasure, but simultaneously realizing the imperativeness of order. Short term pleasure and long term goals stay within the bounds of reality. It has a tough job, serving three masters: the id, the super-ego, and the outside world. As you can well imagine, without a strong and functional ego, a person develops negative stress and discomfort which leads to dysfunctions. In life and society we call them mental disorders.

When creating our characters, understanding the inner conflicts the character has will help us show them to the reader. For example, think of Boromir when he tries to take the ring from Frodo in The Lord of the Rings. Boromir loses control, doing anything to get the ring (id). Then he cries, realizing what he has done, and feeling as if he has ruined everything. He hates himself (super-ego). Strider talks to Boromir as he dies, and Boromir finds peace, understanding that he hasn't failed (ego). The ego balances feelings of greed with feelings of failure and self-hate to gain a rational perspective and peace.

Think about this: how does inner conflict or interiority show change in our characters?

We need to see how Freud saw the id, the ego, and the super-ego in our minds. The ego is the conscious part of our mind. The unconscious mind is where the id and super-ego reside. In Freud's view, the unconscious are things that have been repressed. They constitute what the ego deems necessary to "forget" so a person can survive. The ego keeps the id and super-ego happy.

The ego represses memories, feelings, and thoughts so they don't disrupt our lives. Yet the id and the super ego demand a voice, causing moments of disruption or breakdowns.

Freud held that for problems not to pop up, we must deal with the repressed/unconscious and allow the id and super-ego the spotlight. Let's relate this to writing. Occasionally our characters may act abnormally. Their actions may surprise us. We can help the reader see the driving forces that the character may not yet realize; suppressing a memory of witnessing a murder, being abused as a child, and so on. Writing reveals the necessary. Hinting of suppressed memories instead of telling all. This creates the potential for twists in character development.

Defense Mechanisms

When conflict arises between the super-ego and the id the ego controls the id and super-ego with tools called **defense mechanisms** to protect the self. According to psychoanalytic theory, defense mechanisms exist in the unconscious behaviors of a person. Not all defenses are positive. The majority of people use good strategies to overcome difficult situations. However, everyone also uses unhealthy strategies.

Four categories of defense mechanisms include: Pathological, Immature, Neurotic and Mature. Pathological mechanisms enable an individual to escape from reality. We often view these people as insane or crazy. Immature mechanisms frequent adolescent behavior. When seen in adults, we view them as immature and undesirable while in children they're considered normal behavior. Common among adults, neurotic mechanisms give short term benefits but often cause long term damage. Such as a narcissist coming off as knowing a lot about a subject and impressing people, but later on the narcissist annoys those around him/her and people avoid him/her. Mature mechanisms provide support in short term and long term situations; emotionally strong adults adhere to these mechanisms

Pathological Defense Mechanisms

Delusional projections: untrue beliefs the person clings to no matter what.

Denial: the refusal to believe in external reality because of the extreme threat it poses to the person. Believing something that is inevitable will not happen (e.g. I will never die).

Distortion: the reshaping of external stimuli to fit into one's own internal needs (i.e. irrational thoughts a

person may have about events happening around them).
Example: m

y critique group doesn't know what they are talking about. My story is wonderful. I'm sure I'll get first place.

Splitting: black and white vision; a person who thinks on the extreme and doesn't see the continuum; people are either good or evil.

Immature Defense Mechanisms

Acting out: when a person acts unconsciously to get what they want. We see this in adults who throw fits over things that we see as inconsequential. For example when we see a child throw a tantrum over not getting an ice-cream cone we might shrug our shoulders and at most say the parents need better parenting skills. However, if we see adults throwing tantrums over ice-cream cones, then we'd think that something was wrong with the adults.

Fantasy: when a person withdraws to a fantasy world to deal with problems. Children act out their fantasies at times and, as writers, we do as well. Problems occur, however, when we live in the fantasies we create and no longer deal with real life.

Idealization: when we see others as more than they are. We see a person's qualities and none of his or her faults. Most relationships begin this way. Athletes and rock stars, idolized in today's society, make a good example of idealization.

Passive aggression: gets interesting because a person looks sweet and kind to our face but expresses aggression in ways hard to pin point. Take procrastination for example. Perhaps Jim, a passive aggressive person, procrastinates long enough to cause discomfort for another person, Tom, because Tom took Jim's stapler without asking. Jim fears asking for the stapler back, but he knows if he procrastinates on a project that they both work on then Tom will get reprimanded. This causes anxiety for Tom. Passive aggressive behavior happens when people fear confrontation or lack confidence to stand up for themselves, so they express frustration by passive means.

Projection: when a person takes feelings and thoughts that he or she has and projects them onto others. Extreme jealousy, prejudice, and hyper-vigilance exemplify this. A common example of projection happens when an individual fights against sexual desires (pornography, fetishes, etc.) and tries to create laws to ban pornography because they believe that it is wrong even though they find themselves desiring the act. They project what they feel is right even though it isn't what they want.

Projective identification: when a person projects feelings, thoughts, and behaviors onto another individual. They believe their spouse is unfaithful and having affairs, so they harass the spouse until the spouse finally does, and then they say *I told you so*. Self-fulfilling prophecy. Another example: I believe that others don't love me, so I behave in such a way that others won't love me.

Somatization: feeling negative (upset, frustration, guilt, etc.) about another person. Instead of expressing that negative feeling in a healthy way, a person turns it into a negative feeling toward the self, causing sicknesses, pain, and anxiety.

Neurotic Defense Mechanisms

Displacement: a defense mechanism that shifts anger we feel toward someone or something to another object or person. Dad goes to work, gets yelled at by the boss, comes home, yells at his wife, who then yells at their child, who then kicks the dog.

Dissociation: when a person avoids something (emotionally or physically) that causes overwhelming amounts of stress/discomfort. A loved one dies and the person changes into a happy-go-lucky person to avoid the pain of the death.

Hypochondriasis: the excessive preoccupation about having a serious illness. This sometimes gets an otherwise neglected person some attention. That person visits a doctor, then family and friends get curious and the individual gets the desired attention. About 3% of people who visit primary care facilities suffer from hypochondria and have no actual medical problems.

Intellectualization: a person focuses only on facts, distancing him or herself from emotional aspects of a situation. This combines with isolation and the way a person may detach him/herself from a situation. We see this more in men than women.

Isolation: separation of feelings from ideas and events. A lot of young children I've worked with will just give facts about an abuse, without showing emotion about the event. They separate themselves emotionally so it doesn't hurt. If we distance ourselves from emotions then we no longer hurt. This, understandably, happens often.

Rationalization (excuse making): a person convinces him/herself that all is well, no wrong has been done, using faulty reasoning. A person will make convenient excuses for the situation or behavior; a way individuals avoid responsibility. Nowadays a lot of our children exhibit this behavior and continue to use rationalization as adults. Society gives children excuses such as bad parenting or mental and health problems, valid excuses but if excuses are always provided, these children will likely always use them. For example, ADHD, though a real problem that causes stress in a child's and adult's life, can be manageable in most cases, and with help, the person can succeed. We must know our weaknesses, but also see our strengths and opportunities for success. Rationalization gets used often in stories to show a person going from stagnate to one who succeeds.

Reaction Formation: when we feign a belief opposite of what we believe because the true belief causes anxiety. For example, ultra-religious people hold tight to their beliefs for fear that going against the religious belief will bring them sadness.

Regression: when we revert to childlike states to deal with stressful situations, generally temporary. Example: An individual loses their job and spends all day playing computer games instead of looking for employment.

Repression: widely debated on its validity, occurs when a person forgets or represses a situation; however, the emotions continue with the person. A hypnotherapist uses hypnosis to bring out repressed memories of childhood abuse. Many repressed memories turn out to be false. This casts doubt on the notion of repressed memories.

Undoing: a person 'undoes' a negative thought by doing the opposite. Criticizing a person and then pointing out all the good things about him/her typifies this defense mechanism. Additionally, thinking about killing someone then deciding ways to help them exemplifies undoing.

Withdrawal: a person withdraws from situations or stimuli that cause negative feelings or thoughts. A person no longer leaves the house or makes left-hand turns or so on to stay away from discomfort.

Mature defense mechanisms

Altruism: a person serves others, bringing him/herself pleasure and personal satisfaction. We let go of our own problems and focus on others.

Anticipation: realistic planning for future discomforts. Different from pessimism, anticipation makes plans to overcome difficulties rather than just worrying and expecting the worst. Attitude of planning is key.

Humor: turning difficult topics into funny moments; talking overtly about things in ways that give pleasure to others.

Identification: where we mimic another person. This can be both good and bad. If we emulate our hero's good qualities, then superb, but if we become so enmeshed with the person that we forget who we are, then problems arise. Children need to identify with parents or role models to learn correct ways of social behavior, but they still need the opportunity to be themselves.

Introjection: when a person identifies with an idea or object to the point the object or idea becomes part of them, as simple as picking up sayings from a friend.

Sublimation: when a person changes negative emotions or instincts into positive ones, "Making lemonade out of lemons." As seen in a lot of the books we write and read, turning the weak broken orphan into the heroes of the story.

Thought suppression: when we delay a need or feeling in fear of distracting from a current situation. A person taking an exam suppresses the thought of his/her mother in the hospital in order to concentrate on the exam. Thought suppression also helps a person suppress emotional urges (anger, jealousy, excitement) as well. Thought suppression doesn't signify denial, only allotting an appropriate time and place to deal with the circumstance.

By using defense mechanisms we show our readers why our characters act the way that they do. This gives us the ability to create believable characters that act strangely, yet convincingly because of their defense mechanisms.

Exercise: Using the defense mechanisms above write a scene in which one or more of the defense mechanisms manifests in a character.

Sample Characters

Sarah's defense mechanisms will change throughout the story which will show how she changes. In the beginning she will manifest a lot of the splitting defense mechanism. Seeing only good and evil in people. By the end of the story, after life changing events, her perspective of people will change and she will be able to see the good in people as well as the evil in others. Altruism will play a big role in her life by the end of the story.

Ghiyath uses rationalization and intellectualization to cope with the things that he feels he must do in order to protect his people. His character does not change much throughout the story but the defense mechanism will become more pronounced by the end of the story.

Chapter 4
Schema Theory

Schema theory – developed by Jeffrey E. Young, Janet S. Klosko, and Marjorie E. Weishaar – centers on the idea that we have internal schemas guiding us and making up our personalities. Schemas make up how we think and feel about ourselves and the world around us. Think of your mind as a filing cabinet and schemas are folders filled with various files. We start out with few folders in our cabinet: one day we crawl around and encounter a four legged furry thing which Mama/Dada calls dog, having never seen *dog* before, we trust Mama/Dada. *Dog,* a new object stores away in our filing cabinet in a folder we call animal. We continue crawling around and within a few days we encounter another four legged furry thing and say *dog* Mama/Dada say, "no, cat." The new idea attacks/confronts the schema. We think *dog*, but people we trust say *cat*.

Because we trust them, we add a new file called cat to the animal folder.

Each time our schema gets challenged, we either create a new file for the information, or we change and add to old information. More files and folders, which have been reinforced by good and bad experiences, accumulate over time. The more experiences we have with a particular folder/schema, the more reinforced and harder to change that schema becomes.

When writing about our characters we should incorporate schemas and show how they create our character's personality traits; they could be extreme, but generally aren't. Some stable dichotomous traits include: Labile (easily changed)-nonreactive, Dysthimic (depressed/pessimistic)-optimistic, anxious-calm, obsessive-distractible, passive-aggressive, irritable-cheerful, and shy-sociable. These trait dichotomies lie on a continuum, one on each end and an individual moves on this continuum depending on the situation. We should place our characters on these continuums to understand how they may react in different situations. Make a scale from 1-10 and place each word on either end, then mark where our character fits on each scale.

Schema theory also focuses on coping styles: how people react when they perceive a schema as threatened. The three coping styles –overcompensation, avoidance and surrender – correlate with threat instincts of fight, flight, or freeze.

Overcompensation: People react by believing, feeling, and acting as if the opposite is true. If, for example, a young boy acquires the schema of worthlessness, then as an adult, he tries to do everything perfectly. He appears confident, but underneath, is falling apart.

Avoidance: A person does all they can to avoid a schema, pretending the schema doesn't exist; they won't acknowledge it. Individuals use drugs, alcohol, sex, food, or work addictions in order to avoid schemas.

Surrender: A person does not fight or avoid the schema. Believing in the schema, they feel the pain directly. These passive individuals choose partners who cause the schema to form in the first place. Imagine an individual, Wormtongue, raised by abusive parents. Wormtongue's parents tell him he will never amount to anything and when he argues with them about this they hit him. He learns that if he remains quiet and submissive then he doesn't get hit as much. Wormtongue surrenders to the schema that he is worthless and finds a friend named Saruman who will treat him the way that he has become accustomed to and is comfortable with (the evil sidekick is born).

Schema Theory explores 18 different maladaptive schemas. All of us express these maladaptive schemas to some extent. The extremes of these schemas cause problems. Most healthy characters we create will not express these schemas. Villains, on the other hand, do express these schemas in the extremes. **(Disclaimer: this doesn't insinuate that someone with these schemas are evil, only that villains generally exhibit extreme maladaptive schemas.)** The 18 maladaptive schemas, listed below in Table 2, fall into 5 domain

Table 2:
Maladaptive Schemas

Over vigilance and Inhibition	Other-Directedness	Impaired Limits	Impaired Autonomy and performance	Disconnection and Rejection
Negativity/Pessimism	Subjugation	Entitlement/Grandiosity	Dependence/Incompetence	Abandonment/Instability
Emotional Inhibition	Self-Sacrifice	Insufficient Self-Control/Self-Discipline	Vulnerability to Harm or Illness	Mistrust/Abuse
Unrelenting Standards/Hyper Criticalness	Approval-Seeking/Recognition-Seeking		Enmeshment/Undeveloped Self	Emotional Deprivation
Punitiveness			Failure	Defectiveness/Shame
				Social Isolation/Alienation

Disconnection and Rejection

Abandonment schema: A constant feeling of losing people close, in many different ways e.g. death, mistress, ex-boyfriend, better job offer. A person with an abandonment schema obsesses over signs leading to desertion.

Mistrust/Abuse schema: Denotes people who mistrust others and fixate that people will take advantage of them. They guard themselves from and suspect others. These people resist sharing their thoughts and feelings, distancing themselves from others. Those who overcome this schema learn to distinguish between those they can trust and those they cannot.

In *The Order of the Rose,* my first novel, because of uncontrollable circumstances, a boy flees from his home and later feels abandoned by his parents. Throughout the novel he learns to trust, love, and open up to those trying to help him. He then not only relies on others, but on his inner strength as well.

Emotional Deprivation schema: Common with most clients, but usually goes unrecognized by the person. People feel depressed, bitter, and lonely, not knowing why; expecting others to understand them or nurture them. Individuals with emotional deprivation feel misunderstood, cheated of love, emotionally deprived, a lack of affection from others and yet refuse to ask others for help with emotional needs. They tend to ask questions about others, but skirt talking about themselves and as such neglect the need for emotional support by acting stronger than they feel inside. Due to this lack of support they demand much and get angry when others refuse to give them what they want.

Defectiveness/Shame schema: Individuals feel flawed, inferior, bad, worthless, or unlovable. Feelings of shame about who they are permeate these individual's thoughts and they view any part of them as defective. They worry about others seeing through them and finding out who they irrationally think they are. Typically these individuals devalue themselves and allow others to devalue them; secretly feeling they cause the problems they have with other people. They may seem jealous or competitive. Treatment consists of helping the individual feel a higher sense of self-esteem. Helping them feel worthy of love and respect.

Social Isolation schema: Includes people who feel different from other people. They feel inaccessible to others and may include gifted persons, people with famous backgrounds, or ethnic minorities. Individuals with an extreme social isolation schema stay on the periphery or avoid groups altogether.

We can use the above schemas to help show growth in our characters. If a villain has one of these schemas, then it will give believability to why the villain acts against the society norms.

Impaired Autonomy and Performance

Dependence/Incompetence schema: Defines the childlike, helpless person. Life overwhelms this person and they feel inadequate. They can't make decisions or face change on their own. These people find others, substitutes for parents, to take care of them. They always ask others for help, constantly ask questions while working on projects, seek advice, give up easily, and refuse additional responsibilities. Increasing their sense of competence helps them overcome this schema.

Vulnerability to harm or illness schema: Denotes a person who believes catastrophe will strike at any moment. They feel that something bad, beyond their control will happen and nothing they do will prevent it. These types of people avoid things, become phobic and rely on magical thinking. These people need their expectation of imminent catastrophe lowered.

Enmeshment/Undeveloped self-schema:

Represents a patient fused with a significant other to the extent that their identities blur into one. The person lacks a fully developed self or normal social development. In addition, they believe they cannot survive emotionally without the other or vice versa and drift in the world because of the undeveloped self; feeling guilty for trying to separate from the other. To express their spontaneous natural selves rather than suppressing their true selves is the goal for them.

Failure schema: When people believe that they have failed, relative to their peers, in areas of achievement such as career, money, status, school, or sports. They feel fundamentally inadequate compared to others, inherently lack what it takes to succeed. Two directions this can go: 1) people surrender to the schema and work on everything halfheartedly or 2) they overcompensate and overachieve at everything they attempt. The overachiever, often successful, feels fraudulent and unsuccessful. Many times, failure turns into a self-fulfilling prophecy. These people need help to feel confident and to succeed within the limits of their true abilities.

Impaired Limits

Entitlement/Grandiosity schema: This schema manifests in most people, but not in the extreme. These people feel special - really, really special. They see themselves as better than others, part of an elite group entitled to special rights and privileges. They try, without empathy or concern, to control others to meet their needs. They are excessively competitive, snobby, domineering, manipulative, and forceful in their views.

Insufficient self-control/self-discipline schema: Characterizes people who lack two qualities: 1) self-control – restraint of one's emotions and impulses and 2) self-discipline – the ability to tolerate boredom and frustration in order to accomplish a task or goal (like getting published). ☺ They can't delay short term gratification to achieve long term goals and don't learn sufficiently from experiences, that is, from the negative consequences of their behaviors. In the milder forms, they avoid discomfort. Typical signs: impulsivity, distractibility, disorganization, unwillingness to persist in boring tasks, intense expression of emotions, and habitual tardiness or unreliability. These people need help in giving up short term gratification for long term goals.

The Domain of Other-Directedness

Subjugation schema: These people allow others to dominate them. They surrender control because they fear either punishment or abandonment. Two types exist, subjugation of emotions and subjugation of needs. In emotions, they suppress feelings such as anger. These individuals feel their needs invalidate by or unimportant to other people and act excessively compliant and hypersensitive to feeling trapped. They feel bullied, harassed and powerless. Fear dominates this schema. To help a character with this schema the author would want to show the character seeing that they have needs and feelings; they have the right to express them.

Self-sacrifice schema: Similar to subjugation in that the person tries to meet the needs of others at the expense of their own needs. However, the individual does not sacrifice for fear and although the sacrifice appears voluntary the individual really expects something in return. The individual has good intentions sacrificing their own needs in order to prevent others from experiencing pain, to do what they feel good about, to avoid feelings of guilt or selfishness, or to maintain connection with others. The problem incurs when resentment builds over their sacrifice yielding no reciprocation even though there wasn't any expressed expectation of receiving anything in return. These are characters the reader sees as the "good guys," but who end up joining the "bad guys." Growth in characters with this schema occurs when characters needs are met by either rising resentment turning to selfishness and lack of empathy or by characters learning to express their needs to others.

Approval-Seeking/Recognition-Seeking schema:
People who place extreme emphasis on gaining approval or credit fit in this schema. They obsess over the reactions of others rather than their own reactions. They fail to develop a stable, inner-directed sense of self. Two types occur: one wants everyone to like him/her, and the other wants applause and admiration. They are frequently narcissists. One person with this schema says, "I would rather look like I'm having a good life than actually having one." Individuals with this schema often go out of their way to please others. To overcome this schema an individual would need to learn to recognize the authentic self, and how it's different from the false self.

Over Vigilance and Inhibition

Negativity/Pessimism schema: A person displays a lifelong negative focus while minimizing positives. An individual could learn this schema by the example of the parent or from childhood hardships. A person who develops this schema from experienced loss and hardship at an early age has a harder time overcoming the schema. A pessimistic individual needs help looking at the future more objectively, seeing not only the hard times, but the good as well.

Emotional inhibition schema: People are excessively inhibited in expressing their emotions. Their behavior appears flat, emotionless, and self-controlled without spontaneity; holding back both anger and warmth often exhibiting OCD tendencies and seen as inflexible. A character with the emotional inhibition schema would need help in showing more emotion and spontaneity.

Unrelenting standards/hyper-criticalness schema: These are perfectionists and workaholics. They must reach unrealistically high standards all the time, which the individual internalizes, therefore, they don't change these standards based on others' expectations. They change because they "should," not because they want anything from it. They pressure themselves to achieve. 95% means failure, and second place is the first loser. It's difficult for them and those around them. Helping them accomplish less and to perform tasks not as perfectly can help them overcome the effects of this schema.

An antagonist or better yet a protagonist could easily have this schema. The growth of the characters could center on the characters learning to let go and realizing that they cannot accomplish everything and that they need help from others.

Punitiveness schema: These individuals believe people, including themselves, should be punished harshly for their mistakes. Their actions seem moralistic, intolerant, and unforgiving of their own or others' mistakes. The goal: learn to forgive.

What schema have we incorporated into our stories? And how many of you were saying, "That's me?" (By the way a natural phenomenon while going through a diagnostic course, is to feel like you fit all of the diagnosis.)

Exercise: Pick one or two schemas and write a back story about how the schema formed in a character.

Sample Characters

Sarah does not have a true maladaptive schema; however she does show some of the traits of the unrelenting standards/hyper-criticalness schema. This can be seen by her defense mechanism of splitting which she also uses when she looks at herself. This schema makes it difficult for Sarah to forgive others and herself. Throughout the story she will battle the opposing thoughts of upholding standards and justice and allowing leniency and mercy.

Ghiyath exemplifies the mistrust/abuse schema. Remember one of his characteristics was punctuality due to his parent's unrelenting standards. These unrelenting standards were instigated by the use of physical and verbal abuse when Ghiyath was a young child. As such, Ghiyath learned from a young age that he could not trust others and that he needed to make it on his own. This created another schema within Ghiyath, emotional inhibition. He has learned to show appropriate emotion in social situations but he does not feel the emotion on the inside and those who are around him the most recognize this.

Chapter 5
Human Development

In this section we'll explore different theories on development. We'll review the developmental theories of Freud and Erikson, and then skim through Kohlberg's moral development theory. Finally we'll see how Maslow's hierarchy of needs fits into the picture.

Freud contributed much to modern day psychology and, for many, is seen as the father of psychology. Most work on stages of development start with Freud.

Freud's first stage, the **oral stage**, encompasses birth to 1 year old. The infant fixates on the mouth. Note how infants chew on anything they can fit in their mouths. Most important in this stage is the weaning process. For the first time a child loses something. Here, the child learns about pain and delayed gratification.

If a child does not get through this stage well they become "orally fixated," leading to oral aggression: chewing gum and the ends of pencils, etc.; or to oral passivity: smoking, eating, kissing, practicing oral sex. Oral stage fixation might result in a passive, gullible, immature, manipulative personality.

Freud's second stage, the **anal stage**, lasts from 1 to 3 years old. The key anal-stage experience, toilet training, develops into a battle between the id and the ego. The id wants immediate gratification (not waiting to go to the bathroom) and the ego demands delayed gratification (getting a treat by going potty). The parenting style influences how the child makes it through the experience. Ideally, the child learns the importance of control. If toilet training turns into a bad experience, a compulsive personality may form, for example, a hygiene obsession. Yet if the id wins and parents give in, then the child may form a self-indulgent personality. If parents then fight the self-indulgence the child may develop low self-esteem due to the child acting out the parents' will instead of the ego's will.

Freud considered a person who did not successfully navigate through a stage as psychologically fixated with that particular stage. Consequences of psychological fixation in the anal stage include: 1. Anal Retentive: obsessively organized, or excessively neat; 2. Anal Expulsive: reckless, careless, defiant, disorganized, and coprophilic (abnormal interest and pleasure in feces and defecation).

Freud's third stage, the **phallic stage**, lasts from 3 to 6 years old. The primary area of focus is the child's genitalia. Children explore their bodies and other's bodies with curiosity. The doctor game comes into play during this stage. Exploration helps the child to understand differences, and parents need to teach them acceptable ways to touch so a child won't become embarrassed. Children can develop negative thoughts about their bodies if embarrassment occurs.

The Oedipus complex develops when the son challenges his father for the mother's affection. On the other hand, the girl's complex, called the Electra complex coined by Carl Jung and rejected by Freud, arises when the girl competes with the mother for the father's affection. In this stage Id wants to kill the father because he sleeps with mother, whereas ego attempts nothing, realizing father remains dominate and stronger. Girls develop penis envy, because the anatomical differences make them unable to be with mother, so they turn to father. Freud held that girls experience more stress during this stage than boys.

The defense mechanisms that we talked about earlier begin to form in this stage. During this stage the child learns to relate to the parent of the same sex. Also, during this stage the super-ego forms and the child learns to follow societal rules. Without this, the girl tries to dominate the male by either being overly sexual and/or submissive. The boy will develop an aggressive personality if this stage remains unresolved.

We can use this stage to explain parent/child issues that our characters may have. It also helps us understand the importance of childhood and the differences between healthy and unhealthy upbringings. What if a boy character never knew his father and was raised by an overly possessive mother? Think about the "what if's" in our characters' past.

Freud's fourth stage: The **latency stage** runs from 6 years old to puberty. The ego has no more access to the id because of defenses built up to protect the id. The drive of the id remains hidden or "suppressed" from the ego. The child learns to derive pleasure from secondary resources such as friendships, schooling, family etc. Neurosis, mental disorders involving distress (no longer classified in the Diagnostic and Statistical Manual of Mental Disorders - IV), occurs when a child can't overcome the Oedipus complex or can't derive pleasure in a socially acceptable manner.

Freud's fifth stage: The **genital** stage begins at puberty and continues to death. Criticism about Freud's stages of development highlights his lack of changes after this stage. This stage centers on sexual desires, but with some differences than that of the phallic stage. The individual has a better established ego, and pleasure is no longer the primary-drive of gratification (instinct), but secondary. In other words, pleasure comes in a consensual nature with friendships, love relationships, and family. Unsatisfactory relationships instigate some of the pitfalls of this stage.

Erik Erikson, a developmental psychologist and psychoanalyst, best known for his theory on social development of people and coining the phrase "identity crisis," received training by Anna Freud, the daughter of Sigmund Freud.

Erikson theorized eight stages that human beings go through in life. Each stage made up of opposites, one good the other bad. A person must go through an "identity crisis" in order to move on. A person has a crisis unique to each stage within Erikson's theory. This identity crisis occurs over time and not in a single event.

Erikson's first stage, the hope stage, lasts from birth to 1 year old. An individual must go through the **trust vs. mistrust** crisis during this stage. Infants rely on the parents for their needs such as food, shelter, love, and comfort. The child's understanding of the world comes from the parents. Children comforted, loved, and nurtured in this stage in a dependable manner begin to trust the world. Inversely, if a child lacks these necessities, then they learn to mistrust the world. The children learn whether or not they can trust the world; they must learn trust to overcome this stage.

Think back to the section on schemas and defense mechanisms and about the different schemas and defense mechanisms that would surface in this stage. Think about the characters you create in your books. Were they loved and nurtured as children or were they abused and neglected? Did they learn to trust the world at an early age or mistrust their world? Think about the different strengths/weaknesses they developed from these early experiences. A character struggling in this stage would probably have difficulty trusting those around him/her.

Erikson's second stage, the will stage, runs from 2 to 4 years old and the crisis is **autonomy vs. shame and doubt**. Here children gain more control over their environment. They explore their surroundings. The caregivers need to provide security to facilitate an atmosphere conducive for exploration. The children experiment; touch hot stoves and discover other mistakes in a like manner. The caregivers must provide encouragement for their children. A restrictive parent may instill a sense of doubt and reluctance in the child. On the other hand, if a caregiver encourages self-sufficient behavior, then the child will more likely develop a sense of autonomy.

In order to understand where our character comes from and why they act the way they act we need to understand that character's past. In order to show this to the reader, a writer could use flashbacks, dreams, or a discussion with another character.

Leaders and decision makers don't struggle with this stage, but those who do will follow others. If our main character experienced struggles in this stage, we can show how the character develops self-esteem.

Disclaimer: Keep in mind, as we talk about how parenting influences development, people have individual characteristics, temperaments, and personalities. Caregivers often get a bad rap for poor behavior, but it's not always as simple as bad caregiving.

Erikson's third stage, **initiative vs. guilt**, lasts from 4 to 6 years old. Children become more courageous; they face the complexities of planning and develop a sense of judgment. Risks such as crossing the road alone occur more frequently. Children set goals for themselves. If the goals go unmet, then they become frustrated and show aggressive behaviors such as hitting and throwing objects. When children take initiative to try new things and to venture out, caregivers should encourage the behavior within safe boundaries. On the other hand, children discouraged from taking initiative will begin to feel guilty about their needs and desires.

As children venture out of their comfort zone they will examine the question "Am I good or am I bad?" The caregivers then reinforce one side or the other of the question by how they respond to the child. Supporting children in a caring and loving way, allowing them to make their own mistakes and helping them set appropriate boundaries increases the likelihood the child doesn't face psychological fixation at this stage.

This stage introduces negative aggressive behaviors. Children can reinforce feelings of shame that will follow them throughout their lives. Thinking of the heroes/heroines in our novels we could identify where a caregiver of some sort helped them through a tough time, early on in their lives. Heroes/heroines will have developed intrinsic reinforcement when behaving according to their moral beliefs and their parents see taking initiative as a good thing. In my novel, the hero remembers how his mother and father treated him at an early age. Even though he begins to doubt himself, he remembers this and it helps him through tough times in the story.

What events keep your heroes/heroines going? Experiences as children or later on in life? Think about these questions as the hero/heroine gets stuck in tough spots when most would quit.

Erikson's fourth stage, the **industry vs. inferiority** stage, begins at 7 and lasts until 13 years of age. The adolescent learns to complete productive tasks before desiring play. The children become more aware of themselves and ask "How can I be good?" rather than "am I good?" The child tries hard to act well and responsibly and is more willing to share and cooperate with others. At this stage children can grasp space and time, and they understand cause and effect better. They form moral values, and recognize cultural and individual differences; some may begin to disobey and express their independence.

Erikson saw this stage as critical for the development of self-confidence. Children receive recognition from teachers and other adults and peers. A child praised for attempting or accomplishing good deeds will develop into a more industrious individual, continuing in productive activities. However, if ridiculed or punished for their efforts, they will develop feelings of inferiority. If not allowed to discover their own talents in their own time, a child will develop a lack of motivation, low self-esteem, and lethargy. Children encouraged, not forced, to engage in productive activities to help them discover their talents will develop into healthier individuals.

When creating characters of younger ages, don't make them have insights that they normally wouldn't have. At this stage our characters should begin to recognize their own space and time in society. They should develop their own morals and should veer from the norms, but they won't understand the intricacies that an adult does. Also, adolescents begin to rebel and turn to other adolescents and friends more than their parents for support.

A character unable to make it past the industry vs. inferiority stage will have low self-esteem and will either develop into a recluse or possibly hang with the wrong crowd. Feelings of insecurity will increase the chances that the character will need to make up for those feelings of inferiority by bringing others down and/or usurping power over others.

Erikson's fifth stage, **identity vs. role confusion**, composes ages 14 to 24 years old. The person goes through the "What do others think about me?" phase. They wonder about possible occupations when they grow up, and later they develop a sense of sexual identity. Remember the super-ego. In the past stages the Id had control so we would see a more impulsive individual. Now the child/adolescent/adult thinks more in terms of looking good for others.

Adolescents experience role-confusion as they ponder how to fit in with the adult world. They explore their identity. Erikson proposed that a majority of the adolescents learn their place and find their identity –one of the biggest identity crisis moments of a person's life. Individuals will observe who they have developed into and compare that to what society expects of them. This stage represents the bridge between childhood and adulthood.

The crisis occurs when society insists who the individual should grow into and causes confusion in the individual. If an individual has space to explore and find for themself who they are, then they will gain a strong sense of identity. Of course, boundaries are needed, but allowing the individual to have more space allows for them to discover who they are. The young adult novel falls into this stage giving rise to many conflicts to explore and examine.

Characters stuck in this stage will not know their role in society and may fight or leave the society. Conforming to society's rules will generally increase inner turmoil and stress. Those able to find their way may still fight society, but their reasons differ and they have a stronger sense of identity.

Erikson's sixth stage, **intimacy vs. isolation**, runs from 19 to 40 years old. The person has just passed through the identity vs. role confusion at the beginning and still lingers a little bit into the intimacy versus isolation stage.

The person tries to fit in with the crowd and mold their identity with peers. The person isolates him/herself in some instances due to relationships they form. The person also has fears of possible breakups and rejections.

Once a person forms their identity, they form strong bonds and commit to relationships. The person can then make sacrifices. The main questions, "Am I loved and wanted?" or "Shall I share my life with someone or live alone?"

This stage incorporates more of the books for older readers that we write. The characters experience challenges like marriage, fidelity, children, work, and illness. Commitment to others and sacrifice of their needs for those of others plays a big part of the story. Remember in the beginning of this stage, the main character may still try to find their identity and be more likely to conform, whereas they end up discovering who they have become (generally) and move into the next stage.

Erikson's seventh stage, **generativity vs. stagnation**, composes years 40 to 65. The main question, "Will I produce something of real value?" The person looks to the next generation. The focus no longer revolves around just having children, but on raising the next generation to grow into responsible citizens and on working toward making society better. In contrast, if an individual becomes self-centered and selfish, then stagnation sets in and that person becomes dissatisfied with their relative lack of productivity. Several tasks fall into this stage such as expressing love through more than sexual contact, helping children grow into healthy adults, using leisure time creatively, etc…

This leads me to write about our villains and heroes at this stage. Here we can see Kings and Queens as well.

Also, we can see tyrants. What challenges could we write about in this stage? How much a person changes in this stage and how we show that change in our writing needs investigating. An important question at this stage revolves around change because the character needs to change in order to move into the next stage. Also, a big change would show the change between stagnation and generativity. Scrooge in Charles Dickens's classic, *A Christmas Carol* shows this change.

Erikson's eighth stage, **ego integrity vs. despair**, exists from 65 to death. Here's the question, "Have I lived a full life?" During this stage people tend to slow down and their productivity slows as well. They take more time reflecting, both on accomplishments and on mistakes. If the person sees themselves a success, they develop ego integrity. If, on the other hand, they see themselves as unproductive, they develop a sense of despair. This feeling of despair often leads to depression and hopelessness.

Perspectives change when we feel we know our life nears its end. We often experience denial, anger, bargaining, depression and acceptance. A person thinks about death. Some enjoy and wait patiently while others fight it. Those who have lived good, fulfilling lives tend to face death better.

Think about our characters when they head into imminent danger. Think about what they feel. How they react? Bilbo, in the Lord of The Rings series by Tolkien, makes a good example of going through the stages as he battles between finishing his story and wanting the ring back.

Think about how we see these stages in our lives and in the lives of others and use these experiences to better understand our characters and how they feel through each stage. When you can get into their heads and understand as they understand, we will discover exciting new ways to write about our characters. Feel how our protagonists feel. Empathize with him/her. Use the stages to show the roles that your characters have in your stories, and make them believable.

Exercise: Pick either Erickson's or Freud's stages and write a snippet of how you saw yourself progress through each stage and if you have not reached each stage how you plan to progress through future stages.

Sample Characters

In the beginning of the story Sarah is around 17 which is in the middle of Erickson's identity versus role confusion stage. Sarah will struggle with the concepts of this stage throughout the book, eventually finding her own identity. As the story progresses Sarah's identity will progress as well as she struggles between the expectations of those around her and what she feels she needs and wants to do. Because of the inner strength that she has and the upbringing of her parents, she will prevail.

Ghiyath struggles with the intimacy versus isolation stage even though he is around 45. He remains stuck in this stage because he can't establish good relationships with others and he begins to move towards isolation because of his trust issues that stem from his mistrust/abuse schema. In the story the reader will see Ghiyath continually falling deeper and deeper into himself pushing away from those around him. This will lead into the next stage of generativity versus stagnation where we will see Ghiyath stagnate; remaining a selfish individual.

Chapter 6
Moral Development

This section focuses on moral development and how this affects our characters. First though, we must understand the needs of a person to understand their moral development. Abraham Maslow created a hierarchy of needs in 1943 called *Theory of Human Motivation*; today we know it as Maslow's hierarchy of needs. Take, for example, the song that Tevye sings in *Fiddler On The Roof,* "If I were a rich man." Wealth would allow Tevye to perform the acts he wanted to do, like study the holy book. In other words, by taking care of his basic needs like food and protection, he could then focus more on his spirituality.

The hierarchy starts with the **physiological** level, including breathing, food, water, sex, sleep, homeostasis, and excretion. Maslow proposed that if these needs go unmet, a person will not have desire or motivation to fulfill other needs. More recently, people argue that love falls within a basic need that should be put at this level.

Characters at this level don't worry about how to make the world a better place to live. The concern with finding the basics overwhelms everything else. The *Hunger Games* does a good job of addressing the basic needs of the characters in the story. Kat made it her top priority to find water when first in the arena. She didn't worry about other things, just survival. Think about what happens to people when these needs get neglected, such as during natural disasters, war, terrorist attacks, family violence, childhood abuse, and economic crisis. People no longer worry about laws. They begin to loot or do whatever is needed to care for themselves. When characters get the basic needs met, they start worrying about their safety. **Safety** includes the security of body, employment, resources, morality, family, health, and property. Here characters think about the morals of society.

The next level, **love/belonging**, includes friendship, family, and sexual intimacy. This is an interesting level because, at times (especially in childhood), it overrides the other needs in the hierarchy. An experiment done with monkeys in which a baby monkey had to choose between food and the comfort of a mother showed the importance of this level. The monkey chose the comfort over the food. A very powerful need indeed, when looking at instinct alone. This example should teach a powerful lesson to parents: Children crave attention most.

At this level characters try to build community and family, and concern themselves with their family and friends, protecting those they love. The feeling of belonging to something bigger than themselves plays a large role in their lives.

Esteem, the next level, occurs when a person has confidence and feels achievement in life. The person feels respect for others and respected by others, feeling secure in their relationship with friends and family. Maslow says that this and the following level don't separate but are interrelated needs. These needs relate to how we view others perceive us.

Characters at this level provide support for your other characters because they know what they want and have reached a point in their lives at which they can begin to support others.

Self-actualization is the the highest level a person can attain to. Supposedly, few people reach this level: Mother Teresa, Buddha, Gandhi, Jesus. At times we reach this level and then step down. In fact, many times we cycle through the stages in certain areas, but we eventually step down. However, a person who has attained this level does not step down to a lower level.

A person reaches full potential and understands that potential. This, of course, depends on a person's aspirations and ambitions. Diagram 1 shows the hierarchy of needs.

Diagram 1: Procured from http://ygraph.com/chart/1393

Maslow's Hierarchy of Needs

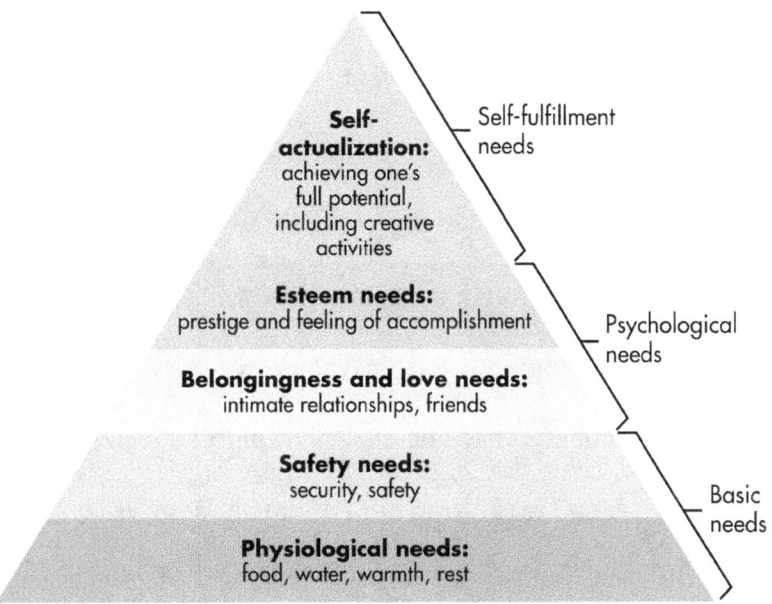

Our heroes have these needs as well as our villains. Raistlin in the *Dragonlance* series realizes what he needs and attains that need. He self-actualizes. Villains have needs, even if others consider them unvirtuous.

Our characters have needs, and as we shape them in our stories, remember the different levels of possible needs. Use the table to guide how your characters grow throughout the story.

Lawrence Kohlberg theorized that moral development has six identifiable developmental stages. Each stage helps a person respond to moral dilemmas. Critics of the theory disagree with justice being emphasized more than other moral values. Nevertheless, Kohlberg's theory reshaped psychology taught today.

Kohlberg tested his theory of moral development on 72 boys, ages 10-16, from both middle and lower class families in Chicago; later on, Kohlberg sampled younger children as well. A problem with this sample was that it was made up of all boys making the findings hard to generalize to girls. Anyway, to ensure inter-rater reliability he also had other researchers test the same children and then compared notes with them. They found a high reliability in the test. Meaning they agreed with each other on the scores given and that they coincided well.

Keep in mind: 1. The stages don't appear as a product of maturation or unfold like a blue print. 2. Kohlberg didn't believe that the stages come about due to a product of socialization. 3. He believed the stages emerge from our thinking about moral problems. In other words, social influences place us into situations where we need to think about the dilemmas and then learn from them. Also, through debates about moral decisions we grow and learn. Further, this can occur when we take on new roles, and we are forced to consider others' viewpoints. Kohlberg believes that the more democratic and open interactions remain, the better the results of moral progression.

Ranking on the scale doesn't evaluate how moral someone's behavior seems, but how a person justifies that behavior. A person's behavior should reflect that person's level of moral development, i.e. the more responsible, consistent, and predictable the person acts the higher the person's moral development. A moral judgment interview, created by Kohlberg, is conducted in order to test where a person resides on this moral scale. The interview takes about 45 minutes and is made up of fictional short stories that describe situations in which a person must make a moral decision. The answers are not as important as why the person chose them.

A sample question from the test:

"A woman was near death from a special kind of cancer. There was one drug

that the doctors thought might save her. It was a form of radium that a druggist in the same town had recently discovered. The drug was expensive to make, but the druggist was charging ten times what the drug cost him to produce. He paid $200 for the radium and charged $2,000 for a small dose of the drug. The sick woman's husband, Heinz, went to everyone he knew to borrow the money, but he could only get together about $ 1,000, which is half of what it cost. He told the druggist that his wife was dying and asked him to sell it cheaper or let him pay later. But the druggist said, "No, I discovered the drug and I'm going to make money from it." So Heinz got desperate and broke into the man's store to steal the drug *for his wife. Should Heinz have broken into*

the laboratory to steal the drug for his wife?

Why or why not?"

Here are some answers that show the different stages.

Stage one (*obedience*): Heinz should not steal the medicine because he would consequently go to prison, which would mean he is a bad person. Or: Heinz should steal the medicine because the druggist overcharges for the medicine. Heinz even offered to pay for it and was not stealing anything else.

Stage two (*self-interest*): Heinz should steal the medicine because he will feel happier if he saves his wife, even if he will have to serve a prison sentence. Or: Heinz should not steal the medicine because prison is an awful place, and he would probably experience more anguish over a jail cell than his wife's death.

Stage three (*conformity*): Heinz should steal the medicine because his wife expects it; he wants to be a good husband. Or: Heinz should not steal the drug because criminals steal not law abiding citizens; he tried everything he could without breaking the law, you cannot blame him.

Stage four (*law-and-order*): Heinz should not steal the medicine because the law prohibits stealing. Or: Heinz should steal the drug for his wife but also take the prescribed punishment for the crime as well as paying the druggist the amount owed. Criminals cannot run around without regard for the law; actions have consequences.

Stage five (*human rights*): Heinz should steal the medicine because everyone has a right to choose life, regardless of the law. Or: Heinz should not steal the medicine because the scientist has a right to fair compensation. Even if he has a sick wife, it doesn't make his actions right.

Stage six (*universal human ethics*): Heinz should steal the medicine, because saving a human life is a more fundamental value than the property rights of another person. Or: Heinz should not steal the medicine, because others may need the medicine just as badly, and their lives are equally significant.

Kohlberg designed his hierarchy into three different levels with two stages in each level. Stage one, **Pre-conventional Morality: Obedience and punishment orientation** characterized by the person believing that powerful authorities have a fixed set of rules that people must follow without question. At this stage the concern centers on what the authorities permit and punish. Characters in this stage have more concern with the law than anything else. They don't ask questions and follow blindly.

Stage two, **Pre-conventional Morality: Individualism and exchange** characterized by people realizing that many different correct views exist. The person understands that different persons have different perspectives. In this stage, the person believes that each individual has the ability to pursue his or her individual interests. Individual's desires determine correctness of a situation or thought. Characters wouldn't worry much about how others act instead these characters carry out what feels good as long as they don't get caught.

Both of these stages fret about punishment. Stage one, punishment ties up in wrongness, whereas in stage two, the concern lies more with the risk that a person wants to avoid.

Stage three, **Conventional Morality: Good interpersonal relationships** reached by most people in their teens. Morality appears as more than just deals. The person believes that they must live up to expectations of others. Interpersonal feelings such as love, empathy, trust, and concern for others arise within the person. In the example from above, Heinz represents uprightness and the druggist "greedy," only thinking of himself. The concept of the loving husband, unfair druggist, and understanding judge comes into play. This refers to conventional morality because the person would normally disagree with stealing, but in special circumstances stealing is okay. Here the person has shifted to a more relativistic outlook.

Stage four, **Conventional Morality: Maintaining the social order**, characterized by a broader understanding of society as a whole, whereas stage three focuses more into the feelings of the individual. The emphasis in this stage centers on obeying the laws, maintaining order at all costs. They look at the example and ask, "What would happen if we all started to break the laws?" Here we see that stage one and stage four answers seem similar but the reasons differ. Stage one looks at only being punished, if I could get away with it. Whereas the person in stage four realizes the importance of the whole. Characters at this level think through the situation with greater depth. These characters look at a situation and make a judgment based on the situation; their answers may vary depending on the situation. In stage three the character will only see the greed of "big brother" or a corporation. They can't see the side of the store owner. While a character in stage four sees the bigger picture and focuses more on society as a whole.

Stage five, **Post-conventional Morality: Social contract and individual rights,** also looks at society, similar to stage four in that the focus revolves around society as a whole. However, in this stage the individual focuses more on the question "What makes for a good society?" Plenty of stories in which utopian societies break down have been written. We can also read religious beliefs on the utopian society. The focus revolves around the responsibilities of society. What rights and values should the society uphold? These people realize the need for a contract between society and its members. They understand that individual groups will have differing views and standards, but they agree on two points. First, they would all want certain basic rights as well as protection. Second, they would want to have a way to change unfair laws through a democratic procedure.

People at this level clarify that individuals should follow laws as a general rule, and that they should protect the laws until they change through a democratic fashion due to their wrongness. They also say that the man in the story has a moral obligation to save his spouse and in fact, to save the life of a complete stranger. In this stage people don't only concern themselves with their own group needs but with the needs of other groups.

The highest stage, **Post-conventional Morality: Universal principle**, builds upon stage five. In this stage we look at all as having universal rights whether the individual belongs to the majority or the minority, this is an egalitarian society. Each party must look through the other's eyes to better understand one another. All parties must be seen as equal, and the people in the groups must consider each situation as if they didn't know which side they would turn up on. In the beginning of Kohlberg's experiment he rated more people at a level six but more recently he hasn't done this as often, finding that people are not consistent in all situations.

For an individual to develop morally, the individual must understand another person's point of view or at least listen to another's point of view. "Don't judge another person until you've walked a mile in their shoes," Atticus said in *To Kill A Mockingbird.*

How can we put our characters into debates to help them change their moral thinking without boring the reader? Can you show change in your character without helping them realize a higher level of moral development? How do our tyrants play into these levels of moral development?

Exercise: Look at the people in your life and find a person that fits into each one of Kohlberg's stages. Write about that person explaining why they fit in that stage and how they got there; the events and experiences that occurred. Keep in mind that Kohlberg believed that an individual arrived at particular stages because of what they thought about during particular social situations. Next, look at where that individual lies on the hierarchy of needs.

Sample Characters

Sarah's story revolves around moral conflicts and how she handles those conflicts. For this reason she will be passing through several different stages until she reaches self-actualization as the leader of a new nation. Beginning in the Conventional Morality: Good interpersonal relationships stage, Sarah will recognize the unlawful acts around her but understand that in order to survive some evils will occur. However, as she runs into more and more people committing unlawful acts she will begin to think about justice and how the injustices are destroying society. This will lead her into the next stage in which she will see the need for order and laws. Here she will begin to establish a society that must conform to the law, allowing little room for mercy. As she sees how the lack of mercy hurts people, she will struggle with the concept of individuals within the society and how their needs are being met, establishing a way that those rules can be changed. Finally, Sarah will reach the final stage in which she will see that all the needs are still not being met. She will further adjust her way of thinking, beginning to see through the eyes of those around her. Sarah will move up and down these stages but still have an upward trend throughout her story.

Ghiyath, on the other hand, sticks to the stage of Conventional Morality: Maintaining the social order stage. Due to his schema he does not have the ability to move above this stage. He focuses on the maintaining of order, even though that order may cause harm to others. By maintaining this order, Ghiyath can rationalize the wrongs that he commits. His defense mechanisms allow him to intellectualize about the problem rather than become emotionally involved.

Chapter 7
Behavior and Perceptions

Behavior

Not only can we observe the physical characteristics of our characters, but we can also observe their behaviors. Ivan Pavlov created a situation in which he conditioned a certain response from dogs: salivation. When the dog heard the sound of footsteps or a bell, it would salivate. First, he used food, an unconditioned stimulus, to cause salivation, an unconditioned response. Second, a neutral stimulus (footsteps) was introduced with the unconditioned stimulus (food) and we got the unconditioned response (salivation). Step three repeats step two over and over. Finally, conditioned stimulus (footsteps) leads to the conditioned response (salivation).

Pavlov then applied this to human behavior to show that we have conditioned responses to certain stimuli. The following example shows how this happens. After my father got home from Vietnam he took a walk down the street and a car backfired, sending him to the ground. People around him didn't dive to the ground because they didn't have the same conditioned response (dive for cover) to conditioned stimuli (loud noise/gun fire). Looking at my father today, we can see how extinction works. My father no longer dives to the ground when he hears a loud bang. He might flinch, but not dive to the ground. A conditioned response (diving for cover) fades when the reinforcement (gun fire) disappears.

We need to understand the different unconditioned responses and unconditioned stimuli that affect our characters, as well as the neutral stimuli that may turn into conditioned stimuli. An example: a character as a young boy experienced the traumatic event of seeing his mother drown. That character now fears large bodies of water because they bring back memories of his mother drowning. Eventually the character will either no longer fear large bodies of water (extinction) or in the extreme, he may never recover from his fear, which we call Post Traumatic Stress Disorder (PTSD).

Protagonists generally have some superhuman ability. They find themselves in some pretty horrible situations and are able to recover. This makes me think of PTSD. Because PTSD happens to some people but not to all who experience the exact same event or circumstance. It raises some interesting questions: why do some people not get PTSD and how do we make it believable when our characters don't get PTSD?

I will do this by sharing a personal experience. When I got into a car accident a couple of years ago, the fear of getting into another accident made me deathly afraid. I had run into the back of another person when they had stopped suddenly. My squishy brakes didn't want to stop that day and so I didn't stop in time. I felt like I had little control over the situation. This of course doesn't mean that I had PTSD, only that my reaction had some similar characteristics that soon wore off. While discussing PTSD with my supervisor we both came up with one of the factors, probably the largest part, control. If a person **feels** like they have control over a situation, development of PTSD following the situation is less likely. The key word is feel. Think about soldiers who go into combat situations and experience high alert for extended time. The majority of them come home relatively okay. But me, in my car crash feared driving because I felt like I didn't have control over the situation. (Like I said, I didn't have PTSD. This is only an example to relate to.)

This brings us back to our Protagonist who gets shot at, thrown into dungeons, faces aliens and dragons, raped, sees loved ones killed before them and many other horrible situations. What makes our protagonist special? Why do our protagonists withstand these situations with little to no adverse effect? Why do they feel in control? Keep this in mind the next time you put your protagonist in a life or death situation.

Watson & Rayner (1920) conducted another study that helps us understand human behavior. The Researchers wanted to find out where emotions come from. They set up the following study: A rabbit was placed in front of a young child named Albert; he didn't fear the rabbit in the beginning. However, later they coupled the rabbit with a loud, scary noise and soon Albert feared the rabbit. This provided support for two of Watson's theories. First, that all human behavior stems from learning and conditioning and second, that behavior stems from unconscious processes.

Watson & Rayner (1920) proposed that behavior generates outside the person. In other words, we learn behavior rather than it being innate at birth. Further, they proposed that we learn our emotions. In fact, he said that everything is learned:

> "Give me a dozen healthy infants, well-formed, and my own special world to bring them up in, and I'll guarantee to take any one at random and train him to become any type of specialist I might select doctor, lawyer, artist, merchant, chief, and, yes, beggar man and thief" (Watson, 1913).

Watson theorized that if presented with a stimulus that produced an emotion, and then coupled with another stimulus, the person would start to equate the emotion to the new stimulus (Just like Pavlov's dog but with emotions).

We can perform our own writing experiments to show how our characters develop. Did they learn it through the course of their life or did your character have the characteristics from birth? Do they have a strange response to something due to past stimuli? What about smells? Do they get happy when they smell Christmas trees? Also, this helps us better understand why a character fears a certain situations that another would shrug off.

Another study conducted by Bandura, A., Ross, D., & Ross, S. A. in 1961 investigated how aggression came about: was it innate, or was it transferred from one subject to the next (learned). The researchers proposed that if a child saw an adult acting aggressively, that child would "learn" that behavior and do likewise. During the experiment a child went into a playroom where an adult would then enter to beat up on a Bobo doll. Other children, the control group, had an adult come in who didn't beat up the Bobo doll. The experiment included both female and male models. The children then went to another room which had toys and the Bobo doll available to play with. The researchers observed the children through a one-way-mirror in which the researchers noted each act of aggression displayed by the child.

The children exposed to the violent acts imitated the acts they had seen by the adult. Boys' violent behavior was more influenced by the male model than the female model and boys showed more violent acts than girls.

This study showed that through observation, violent ones in this case, children could learn behaviors. They also showed that male aggression appeared more acceptable than female aggression. Understanding that behavior is learned through observation, our characters can act in the same manner. Much depends on the societies we build within our stories to make our stories realistic. When we have models for our characters, especially ones seen as authority figures, we need to show how the model's behavior affects the character. Do we have an "evil" model for our character? If so, does that character learn the behavior or parts of the behavior? Maybe the character transforms into the hero of our story, but has hints of behavior from the "evil" model. Maybe the main character has to stop from killing someone as he flashes back to the cruelty of his father. Which sex dominates our society? How about a female character? If she either walks away from a fight or tries to defend herself how do others view her?

The learned behaviors that our character exhibit, and how the models around them affect their behavior explains to our readers the world the character lives in.

Show the reader that the characters in our book have learned some bad and good behaviors from those around them.

Perceptions

We have senses: hearing, feeling, smelling, seeing, and tasting. Our mind constantly takes in, processes and tries to understand these five senses. Pause for a moment and think of something we sense with all five senses. I'm always amazed at how much we sense and how much our mind ignores. Our perceptual processes do four general things: selects the senses to pay attention to, organizes these senses, interprets this organization and makes sense of the world.

The brain uses several tricks to make sense of our perceptions, one being Figure-Ground, where we focus in on one thing and ignore the rest.

What do you see when you look at the above picture? Do you see a young woman or an old woman or both? Perceptual Constancies know and perceive objects the same, even though our senses give us new information about the object. For example, as you walk around a chair, the senses tell you new things about the chair, but you still see it as the same object. Size Constancy gives the ability to tell that when five blocks away from a bus, a person still sees it as a full size bus.

Once again the question of learned versus innate arises (nature vs. nurture). In order to understand whether perception arises from nature or nurture, Colin Turnbull studied a man who lived in a jungle. When the man leaves the jungle, he sees for the first time, a mountain that stands a long distance away. He doesn't know how to comprehend the mountain and can't tell the difference between a mountain and a cloud. Seeing a buffalo from a long way, away the same man wonders what kind of insect he sees. He hasn't learned how to perceive size constancy outside of the jungle where everything is up close.

In applying this to writing, first we need to understand the senses around us: sight, sound, touch, taste, and smell. Second, when writing about our characters going into new environments and places, we need to know how they react based on their perceptions of those new places. Can they comprehend the things around them? Next, think about how other characters perceive our characters. Do they see them as handsome, smart, ugly or lazy? How do those perceptions of our characters correspond to the perceptions that our characters have for themselves?

Understanding our character's behaviors and perceptions will help us envision how our characters behave and interact with other characters in our story.

Exercise: Take five minutes a day to focus on your senses. What do you hear, smell, feel, see and taste? Do this in different environments and during different activities. Perhaps you have just made a delicious meal. Take the time to savor the flavors as they touch your tongue. Where do you taste those flavors on your tongue? What does it smell like? Go to a park, a ball game, a mountain top. Write down these experiences and compare them to the emotions you felt at the time.

Sample Characters

Sarah grew up in an environment that had little to no violence. She experienced a peaceful childhood with good parents who taught and treated her well. The experiences in childhood have molded her behavior to react in a positive manner. When faced with despair and defeat, she reacts by working harder. Perceptions are often seen through rose tinted glasses. In order to show growth in her character, her story will take her to the point of breaking and perhaps beyond so that the inner self can see conflict and turmoil, increasing her personal growth.

Ghiyath's behavior reflects that of his childhood which was filled with pain and feelings of abandonment. His parents ruled the country before him and as such they were very busy, leaving him to be raised by others. His parents would often use physical punishment to make their point, showing little love and affection. In turn Ghiyath treats those around him in the same way. He rules with an iron fist, enacting his will without regard to others. However, he still understands the merit of intrigue and subterfuge. This allows him to behave kindly and respectfully to those he tries to bend to his will. He has a jaded perception of those around him. He believes others are out to get him and to take from him what rightfully belongs to him. He appears happy on the outside, but at times his inner turmoil causes him to become deathly sick.

Chapter 8
Culture/Social influences

In diagnosing characters we need to take several uncontrollable factors into account, such as cultural and social influences. To cover this subject in this book would be impossible due to the enormity of the subject. That being said, this section should give a little background into things to think about while diagnosing our characters.

Two individuals come together in order to create a child (no, I'm not going to talk about the birds and the bees), a man and a woman. (A child born on the distant planet x5957, may have a different process of coming about. In that case, the author will have to think of who or what influences the character.) When born the child comes from two individuals with unique characteristics that will make up the child in a unique manner. These characteristics, of the child, develop and change not only by how the guardians raise the child, but also by the environment that the child knows. A huge debate among theorists encompasses the question of what influences a child more: nature or nurture.

Within the question of nature versus nurture another debate arises: how much does parenting influence a child. Many studies have examined the effects of parenting and a majority of people accept that parenting does in fact influence the outcome of a child. In the process of these studies, a common theme has developed, known as parenting styles. Maccoby and Martin, in 1983, developed a theory that included four parenting styles: Authoritative/Propagative, Authoritarian/Totalitarian, Indulgent/Permissive, and Neglectful which will be discussed further along in the chapter. Table 1 shows the development of these styles.

Table 1

Four Parenting Styles:

	Un-Demanding	Demanding
Responsive	Indulgent/Permissive	Authoritative/Propagative
Un-Responsive	Neglectful	Authoritarian/Totalitarian

All parents will fall into all of these different areas throughout their parenting experiences, falling within the authoritative/propagative area most of the time. Generally speaking, parents love and care for their children and want the best for them.

When looking at the parents of characters, we don't always run into loving, healthy adults. More likely we will run into the Dursleys or the evil stepmothers. Why do children have such horrible parents in books? Or, on the other hand, the most wonderful parents (e.g. the Potters)? The different types of parents created for our characters are one thing that can provide an additional element to our story (e.g. motivation, strength, conflict).

A study, by Harry Harlow, in the 1960s conducted several controversial experiments on rhesus monkeys. The object was to prove that newborns need more than just food and shelter. They also require love and affection. In his experiment, he took newborn rhesus monkeys from their mothers and put them in cages with two different surrogate mothers; one a wire monkey that had a milk bottle attached to it, so the monkey could eat. The other a terrycloth monkey, providing warmth and a kind of affection. The experiments showed that the monkeys spent much more time with the terrycloth monkey, even though it provided no food. Now this cruel experiment clearly proved the importance of love and affection to the newborn rhesus. The experiment also showed that without this warmth and affection, the monkeys developed psychological problems and some even died from the trauma. (Orphanages in Eastern European countries, with too many kids, have similar results.)

Harlow further pointed out that the key to successful parenting includes contact comfort. In creating our characters, we need to understand where our characters get their contact comfort from, how this affects our characters, and if they have had too much or too little. We need to understand that different characters may need more love and comfort than other characters. All of our characters need some form of comfort and love.

The Neglectful Parent

The neglectful parent, also called the hands off, detached, uninvolved, or dismissive style, completely ignores their child. They don't even make the effort to discipline their children. Personal issues of the parent overwhelm the parent to the point that they don't have time for their children. Children not only have no limits set upon them, but they also have little to no warmth provided by their parents. Some of these parents can provide the basic necessities for the child, but don't provide emotional support. Parents addicted to drugs make up some of the worst cases of this style. The children, from a very young age, must learn to fend for themselves.

Children that have these types of parents generally develop a sense that other aspects of the parents' lives come before them. Many of the children develop patterns of truancy and delinquency. They detach from society and have problems with forming good relationships in the future. Some children may become overly attached to others and very needy or the opposite: They need no one. They may also hoard food. One child, who went to a better home, after being neglected, would store food under his pillow and bed for many years, even though the family provided plenty of food and love. Important note: parenting does not influence everything in the formation of a child's personality. In fact, many may argue parenting plays a very small role.

Many well-adjusted people have come from neglectful families. Do they still have issues due to the neglect? Yes, but they have learned to overcome them, move on, and succeed. Nothing is absolute!

We must realize that our neglected characters will have issues. They will likely have problems attaching to others, trust issues, and they may turn out as villains. This brings us back to our question of why parents in books and movies act so terribly. In the case of the neglectful parent, it provides a challenge that the child, or later adult, in our stories must triumph or fail to overcome. The parenting style gives the reader an explanation for the character's action.

Most of us can empathize with a person who has gone through neglect and suffering. If our main character has a history of neglect, the reader will feel that much more excitement when the character overcomes all. The success of the character inspires hope in the reader and creates an emotional bond between the reader and the character.

The Authoritarian Parent

This style probably fits best with the super ego thought process, if comparing to Freud's work, due to the fact that the law must be followed, no matter what. We must be strict, and the child must behave and follow every order.

The authoritarian parent demands perfection but doesn't respond to the emotional needs of the child. In the extreme case, totalitarian parenting: my way or the highway, no ifs, ands, or buts, the parent expects children to conform to their rules with little to no open dialogue between parent and child. Expectations of the child run high with few if any explanations and little reasoning for the rules and boundaries. Due to this parenting style, the child will generally have less social competence because they have been told how to act and respond; the parent doesn't give the child room to make choices. Further, these children will often rebel, break down, or run.

If you want a character that has bad social manners or who submits easily and readily, then show the reader this type of parenting style. Also, this parenting style could explain why a character runs away from his family. Generally, these characters will either be broken/submissive or the complete opposite, totally rebellious against any type of authority. Doormats and anarchists make up this group.

The Indulgent Parent

The Indulgent parent, also known as permissive, non-directive or lenient, feels like they should always say *yes* and never *no* to their children. Demanding little or nothing from the child and responding to all of the child's needs/wants no matter the cost, the free-range parent where anything goes. These parents nurture and accept their children, but do not teach them limits. They support their children and most people see them as great parents. However, the children don't learn to regulate themselves or behave appropriately. The child tends to end up being a spoiled brat or spoiled sweet depending on the behavior of the child.

So what happens to these kids? A recent study found that children who have indulgent parents have nearly triple the risk of participating in heavy drinking. In comparison, children with strict parents have double the chance of heavy drinking. Additionally, children that have the indulgent type of parents tend to be more impulsive, and as adolescents, may engage in more misconduct and drug use. These children have a hard time learning to control their behavior and emotions; they always expect to get their way. On the other hand, these kids may turn out to have better emotional security, more independence, and mature quicker.

How would these characters look in our books? A pampered princess in the castle comes to mind; who for whatever reason, leaves the castle and meets the rugged hero. She learns to live on her own with the help of the hero and changes from a weak dependent woman into an independent heroin who defends her homeland in the end.

The Authoritative Parent

The authoritative parent, also called the assertive, democratic or balanced parent, both demands from and responds to the child. This parenting style centers on the child and holds high expectations of maturity of the child. Understanding of the children and looking for ways to help them with their problems is key. They emotionally support them. Rules, boundaries, and consequences for those rules, if broken, get discussed between the parent and child. They allow verbal give and take. These types of parents don't control, allowing their children to explore, allowing the child to mature and learn to make their own decisions.

Further, these parents have expectations for their children, unlike the permissive parent.

When giving out punishments, the child knows why they are punished and what the parents expected. Parents are attentive to the child's needs, and in some instances will forgive and teach when a child falls short.

Children generally have a higher self-esteem and independence. We generally won't see these children in the principal's office, jails, or counseling centers. This doesn't mean that these children will turn out perfect; they still may have many other situations that come up in their lives that will cause problems. It only means they have the support needed to get through life's challenges.

In a novel that I wrote, the main character had great parents and when conflicts come up for him, he recalls memories of his parents in order to survive the tough times. Like my character, other characters with authoritative parents will have an inner strength that gets them through dark times.

Using parenting styles in diagnosing our characters, offers a great tool to explain and expand upon our characters' actions and backstories. Parenting styles allow us to put our characters through terrible situations and explain why our characters make it through them and help us gain sympathy from our readers. By showing the interactions of our characters and their parents, we create a story that our readers can relate to and understand, drawing them into our worlds and capturing them, leaving them craving more.

Peer Pressure

Solomon Asch conducted several tests, during the 1950s, examined how peer pressure influences conformity. Asch wanted to see if peers could influence individuals in giving incorrect responses. The experiment involved 8 people sitting around a table with only one of them as the actual subject, the rest were confederates. The 8 participants answered a simple question of which line was longest or which line was similar to a reference line. The confederates would, at first, give correct answers, but then give incorrect ones, to see how much their answers influenced the subject.

The results showed that peer pressure could have a measurable influence on answers given. In the control group, where everyone gave the correct responses, the subject gave only 1 incorrect response out of 35. On the other hand, when "peers" gave incorrect responses over one third of the subjects gave incorrect responses. At least 75% of the subjects gave the wrong answer to at least one question when the "peers" gave incorrect responses. Figure 1 shows an example of one of the pairs of cards used in the experiment. A question from the study would look something like, "which line is equal to the reference line? A,B, or C." The card on the left has the reference line and the one on the right shows the three comparison lines.

Figure 1: Example of the cards used.

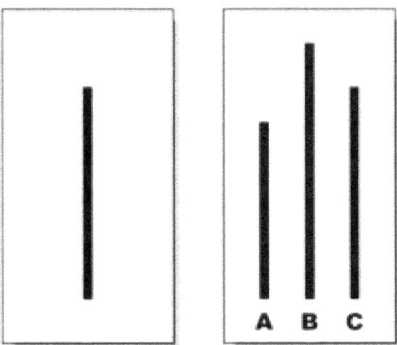

Follow up experiments showed that with more confederates, the more forceful a difference in the results. One confederate made little difference but influence increased as two or three joined in. However, if one confederate disagreed with the other confederates it improved the likelihood that the participant would choose the right answer.

This study shows that people can easily pressure peers into doing things, even if they know that what they get pressured into goes against their moral beliefs. People want to fit in. Very few people want to stand out from the crowd. In fact society generally punishes those who stand out. In diagnosing our characters, we should evaluate what kind of character we have. A character who leads or follows? Just because your character leads doesn't mean the character will never fall for peer pressure and do something he wouldn't normally do. Readers will not believe a character if the character always goes against the crowd. If the character conforms occasionally, it will draw the reader in. We've all experienced peer pressure.

Obedience to Authority

In 1961 Stanley Milgram conducted a study to see how far a person would go to obey an authority figure; he wanted to understand why Nazi soldiers did horrible things during World War II. The question of the study, "Was it that Eichmann and his accomplices in the Holocaust had mutual intent, in at least with regard to the goals of the Holocaust?" In other words, did those involved have a mutual sense of morality? The results from his study suggested that the millions of accomplices just followed orders.

In the study, the participant went into a room with another person (in reality this person was an actor and accomplice to the study) and told that they would be helping that person (actor) learn by shocking them when they made a mistake. The participant could see the actor through a one way mirror and was told that the 'student' (actor) on the other side of the mirror couldn't see them. The instructor told the participant that if the 'student' answered the question incorrectly, the participant must shock the 'student' and for each incorrect answer the amount of shock would need to increase. As the 'student' received shocks, he began to complain of heart problems, even banging on the wall sometimes. Most participants said they wanted to check on the 'student,' but the instructor in the room with the participant assured the participant that they wouldn't get in trouble or held liable and that they must continue the test. If the instructor gave four verbal prods and the participant still wanted to stop, the experiment would stop. Otherwise, the experiment would continue until the participant had administered 450 volts (a lethal shock).

The results showed that 65 percent of the participants administered the full voltage. That means 26 out of 40 of the participants would have killed a person when instructed to do so by an authority figure. They all questioned what they did, but they kept going nevertheless. Milgram said, "Stark authority was pitted against the subjects' (participants') strongest moral imperatives against hurting others, and, with the subjects' (participants') ears ringing with the screams of the victims, authority won more often than not. The extreme willingness of adults to go to any lengths on the command of an authority constitutes the chief finding of the study, and the fact most urgently demanding explanation."

You may think that this kind of thing wouldn't happen in today's society, or we would never follow authority like that. However, recently Jerry M. Burger in 2009 replicated the Milgram studies. You can actually view the experiment on YouTube. Burger's experiment had similar results to the Milgram study, showing that even today in our "highly sophisticated" society we still conform to what authority tells us to do.

People follow many different authorities: a person, an institution, a country, or even an idea. Think of how blindly we follow what our doctors tell us to do, or when we watch something on the news and believe it without questioning. Students follow professors without question. Even this book, many will accept without checking the facts.

This experiment shows us a lot about human nature and authority. We need to ask ourselves, why does our character buck the system and go against authority? What makes our character special? By answering these questions we define our characters. If unanswered, your reader will lose interest in your character and your story develops into an unbelievable tale that few will buy into.

The Stanford Prison Experiment by Phillip Zimbardo (1971) expands upon the Milgram study and sees how people would take on the role of authority and how far they would take it. The participants included 24 undergraduate students – half assigned as guards, the other half prisoners. Zimbardo selected these participants because of their characteristics of having no criminal background, psychological or medical problems. The setting: a mock prison in the basement of Stanford University. In the experiment Zimbardo acted as the warden. Zimbardo wanted the experiment to last for two weeks.

The results showed how easily authority can engulf a person and quickly become abused. The guards acted so inhumane and abusive, the study ended in six days rather than the scheduled 14 days. Many of the prisoners showed signs of extreme stress and anxiety. Five of the prisoners experienced such extreme problems that they discontinued the study earlier than 6 days. The experiment even affected Zimbardo to the point he couldn't see how the experiment affected the participants. In fact, the study probably would have continued had a friend not informed him of the problem and told him to end the experiment. Essentially the guards developed aggressive and abusive personalities while the prisoners became passive and depressed.

This study shows how power corrupts people and when granted, people do things that they normally wouldn't do. Also, this study shows what happens to people put into adverse situations (prison) and not only how they will react, but how short a time it takes for them to break down. This makes me think of criminals. How do they withstand the same psychological breakdown, or do they? Have they, perhaps, already gone through the process at some earlier time in their lives and learned to survive and cope with the situation?

Our characters need to have something that keeps them from breaking. Do they have an inner resolve to do what their inner moral compass tells them to do? Do they continue because of the support of others? Does a belief in a higher power give them the resolve to continue even though the future looks grim? Do they grow accustomed to the situation by slowly immersing into the situation (the frog in boiling water)? What makes them so resilient when the vast majority of us would break? Or do they break and because of that break change forever and, resolve to do better etc.?

These experiments explain a lot about human behavior and how people will react under difficult situations and how authority and power affect us.

Answering the questions asked in this section will increase the believability of our character and bring him/her to life. Our heroes and heroines step out of the norm. Those corrupted by the power make our villains just as believable.

Culture

Culture plays a huge role in who we become and how we behave. Whether we go against the cultural norm or we follow it, culture still influences us. This is true of both the culture we were raised in and the one that we currently occupy. Cultural influences: interpersonal attraction, sex, touching, personal space, friendship, family dynamics, parenting styles, childhood behavior expectations, courtship rituals, marriage, divorce, cooperation vs. competition, crime, love, and hate. I encourage that we to look at our cultures and their influences on how we act.

A person can have cultures within cultures. For example, a person may live in America (1), live in a particular state (2), within a county (3), within a city (4), within a particular part of town (5), within a family unit (6). This doesn't even take into consideration the religion of the family, did they move recently or live in the same place their entire lives, and other similar factors.

Triandis et al. (1988) proposed that culture contains different dimensions. Whether or not an individual belongs to an individualistic or collectivism culture makes up one dimension. The team listed several differences between the two types, and then began conducting studies on them. The team considered the following attributes to come from a collectivist culture: sacrifice, self as an extension of group, group is paramount, greater conformity, "vertical relationships" (child-parent, employer-employee) valued more, shame, hide interpersonal conflicts and others. The team believed that individuals from an individualistic culture would have the following attributes: Hedonism, self is distinct from group, self-reliance is paramount, less conformity to norms, greater value on money and possessions, preference to confront interpersonal conflicts, horizontal relationships (friend-friend, husband-wife) valued more, guilt and others.

These two types of culture make up opposite extremes, and individuals and cultures will generally lie between these two extremes. When creating our world for our character, understand the culture(s) that influence the character. How does it look? What does the culture expect of the character? What happens when someone goes against the culture?

Along with culture comes prejudice. In an experiment known as the Robbers Cave Experiment, conducted by Muzafer and Sherif 1954, researchers looked at prejudice in social groups. The experiment was conducted in a 200 acre summer camp surrounded by the Robbers Cave State Park in Oklahoma. The participants in this study included 24 twelve-year-old boys with similar backgrounds. The researchers divided the boys into two groups with twelve boys in each, and then loaded the boys onto two separate buses. During a 1 week period the boys camped in two separate areas in the camp. The study had 3 phases in all: In-group formation phase, Friction phase, and an Integration phase.

Within days of first contact the boys from each group developed hostilities towards the other group even though they had not known each other previously. Further, observers observed name calling and derogatory songs from each of the groups towards the other group. The friction phase commenced but ended quickly because the boys turned hostile toward each other. The researchers believed the boys would hurt one another, making the experiment unsafe to continue, so phase three commenced. To see how two groups could come together even after the formation of prejudices the experiment had an integration phase. In this phase, the researchers used activities that required both groups to work together in order to complete certain tasks. The two groups learned to work together and soon the boys formed good friendships, to the extent that they all insisted on riding home together on the same bus.

Lord of the Flies uses themes comparable to this experiment. The idea is that in-group hierarchy takes place as well as out-of-group hierarchy. In realistic conflict theory, inter-group conflict arises between groups as they compete over the same limited resources. Muzafer and Sherif suggest that this could be a possible cause of prejudice and discrimination.

This experiment not only showed the effects of prejudice and how it forms in a short amount of time, but also how prejudice could dissolve and be overcome when the two groups have to work together.

What does the hierarchy of our societies look like? Where do our characters fit into this hierarchy? How does it affect them? What motivates our characters to change the society they reside in?

Society vs. The Individual

What has more importance, the society that a person resides in or the individual? Individuals and groups ask this question over and over in ethics classes, research, lawmaking, and in any other situation that involves placing either society or the individual over the other. In a fictitious vignette about a study on cancer, the researchers studied a hypothetical drug that cured most kids but made others worse and some even died. All of the kids were terminally ill. The question came up, do we stop research because of the few terminally ill children that die sooner than expected, even though the drug benefits and saves most of the others? Society or the individual? Does it make it okay to hurt a few in order to save the majority?

When we create our characters we need to understand the character's viewpoint on this. We need to know what they would do in certain ethical dilemmas. Would they stop the study because of the harm being done to the minority or would they continue because the benefits outweigh the loss? This can influence how they react in certain situations. Will they forget the world because of the dire trouble their family faces or will they say the world comes before my family? This conflict of family versus the world gets used over and over in stories. The villain puts the hero in a situation in which he can only save one, society or his love.

Exercise: Put the main character of your current work in progress (WIP) in several hypothetical situations in which they need to make ethical decisions. Make sure that the characters can't solve the dilemmas too easily, but are difficult enough to help you evaluate the values of your character. Then afterward, evaluate why they chose the way they behaved. The why will illuminate the character as much or more than the decision itself.

Sample Characters

Sarah belongs to a religious family that lives in the north subdivision in the town of Apple Valley. Apple Valley belongs to the south region of the People's Collective which makes up part of the Northern hemisphere of the planet Eorthe.

The culture in Apple Valley predominately revolves around the religious belief that if you follow the commandments found within the holy book, then the people will prosper. Those who fight against this belief are allowed their right to believe as long as it does not interfere with those around them. Advanced technology also plays a large role in the society. All of the homes and buildings use solar panels to supply energy. The homes have what we would consider advanced features such as automatic temperature adjustments, window shielding, projectors and other conveniences and entertainment needs. Apple Valley lies in a farming community and as such has a small town feel to it. The people do not worry too much about outside politics and try to stay to themselves. This however has become increasingly more difficult as outside influences have been pressuring the town to supply more water to surrounding metropolises. Apple Valley city council wants to play a bigger role in the politics of the People's Collective, however Sarah's parents want to leave the collective alone and retain more of their independence. The People's Collective believes that the society as a whole takes precedence over the individual.

The biggest discrimination between the people revolves around social economic status (SES). Those of lower SES are unable to move up within the power structure. This does not mean that the discrimination is obvious. There are welfare programs and other supports for the lower SES and an appearance of movement.

Sarah fits within the middle class and has a comfortable life. She does not have everything but has her needs met and enjoys many different entertainment activities. Her family generally goes against the beliefs of those around her and has not succumbed to peer pressure. They believe in some of the religious beliefs and attend church meetings but her family also believes in some of the older traditions that are no longer practiced by the rest of the religious group.

For the most part Sarah's parents fall under the authoritative parenting style. The rules of the house get discussed and negotiated as well as the consequences of those rules. Being the oldest, Sarah has learned to show an example of the rules and has helped in changing and managing those rules. She has gained responsibility and a strong sense of being due to how her parents have raised her. This gives her an inner strength that she can call on in time of need.

Ghiyath's family has recently come into power and he currently reigns over the populace of Barbadras in the desert region of Barakah. The city Barbadras trades with many of the surrounding cities and is known for its advanced technology. Even though the city has advanced technology, it lacks the ability to control the power granted by the five Gods. Due to their lack of controlling ability a fragile balance remains between the differing cities in the region. However, that balance begins to shift in the beginning of Ghiyath's story as Babadras has grown in strength.

Barbadras culture revolves around the gladiator pits. The ruling class uses the pits to punish those who fight against them and to give entertainment to the masses. Slavers will go to faraway places to capture exotic beasts and humanoids. They have also been known to kidnap young children and even entire families at times from the surrounding towns.

Ghiyath heads a governing board that rules over Barbadras. Ghiyath's family has slowly been taking more and more power from the ruling body and currently the ruling body is more of a figure head than anything else. The general public does not perceive the power struggle.

Chapter 9
Cognitive and Emotional Aspects of our Characters

Cognition

Rene Descartes, a French Philosopher, probably best known for his statement: Cogito Ergo Sum, I think therefore I am. There must be an "I" doing the thinking therefore "I" exist. We have talked about the idea of behaviorism and a few behavioral studies that look at stimuli as motivators behind everything we do. In behaviorism, a person can observe behavior directly, including the antecedents to the behavior, and what came after the behavior. Behaviorists know this as the ABCs (Antecedent, Behavior and Consequence). During the 1930s and 1940s, everything was examined this way. Behaviorists gave little to no thought to unobservable behaviors, such as thinking and feeling.

Tolman, E. C. 1948 known as the father of cognitive behaviorism proposed that not only do humans and animals think, but that this thought can be observed, if indirectly. He created rat maze experiments that proved this point. He said that we have cognitive maps that help us get from point A to point B even if we have to navigate blocks placed in our usual path. So imagine heading to your local grocery store and construction blocks your normal path. Most of us would have the ability to determine an alternate path. A cognitive map works in this way.

Through Tolman's experiments, we learn that we don't just respond to stimuli, but we will actually think through what happens to us, and we can adjust our behavior depending on what we observe around us. We do not just respond to stimuli, but actually go through the process of evaluating and thinking about the stimuli to come up with the best alternative.

Tolman then expanded this idea to thoughts on society. If a person has a narrow strip map, meaning they have little perspective or don't think beyond the construction then they can develop prejudices toward others because they can't think outside their own understanding. While on the other hand, if a person has broad strip maps and can expand their thinking and include, or at least understand, other ways of thinking, they will not show prejudice toward others.

Our characters also need to think through situations and understand the broader meaning of what happens around them rather than just reacting to stimuli. A character that doesn't think, but just reacts to everything around them will appear as a flat puppet. For this reason we should show the thoughts of our characters. A writer can do this through the behavior of the character, such as a pause; or more directly by writing out the thoughts of the character also known as interiority.

Another important study of how we think, conducted by Gazzaniga, M.S. in 1976, examined how the two halves of the brain worked. He looked at patients who had their corpus callosum (the structure that connects the right and left hemisphere of the brain together) surgically cut. Surgeons would do this as a treatment to prevent or reduce seizures in people with epilepsy. By conducting tests on these patients Gazzaniga could see how they responded to different tests.

He found that the left hemisphere of the brain has superior speech compared to the right while it seemed visual-spatial abilities appear more proficient with the left hand. This means that visual-spatial abilities tie into the right hemisphere of the brain; some parts of our bodies such as our hands actually connect to the opposite side of our brains. Further, other parts of our brain connect to emotions while some are connected to thinking.

The more that we as authors understand the brain and how it works, the more we understand characteristics of our characters. Perhaps a character gets clubbed in the back of the head and goes blind for a day or two; the rear part of our brains processes sight, so this would be logical. Understanding how strokes affect people makes up another example of how understanding the brain can help us in writing. One consequence of a stroke called Broca's Aphasia causes a person to lose the power to use or comprehend words; this occurs due to Broca's area being damaged. Broca's area is a tiny area of the brain that controls language. Certain techniques used by the person affected by Broca's Aphasia help the person overcome this disorder, but the brain also does its part in compensating and correcting the problem.

When looking at the brain and how we think we should also consider the concept of memory. Two different types of memory exist: cognitive memory and emotional memory. Memory allows us to store, retain, and recall information. The shortest type of memory, called sensory memory, occurs when we see something for 200-500 milliseconds. Even through rehearsal it can't be remembered, the person can see or sense something but can't recall the object. The second, short term memory, can be remembered if rehearsed. Whatever the person rehearses develops into long term memory and those things that a person doesn't rehearse remain in short term memory for a few seconds to a minute then is lost. It has been found that an individual can remember up to 7 ± 2 numbers. However, when using a technique called chunking, the individual can remember an increased amount of numbers (the reason why phone numbers have splits). The third type of cognitive memory, long term memory, lasts the lifetime of the individual. The brain has an infinite amount of space to store information. Keep in mind as we write our characters that different injuries, illness and other accidents can affect memory.

"Why do we forget?" Sigmund Freud wrote a book called *Psychopathology of Everyday Life.* In this book, he writes about the different reasons people forget things such as names, foreign words, and order of words. He breaks down different instances, in which either he or someone he talks to forgets something, to try and figure out why they have forgotten the particular thought or memory. Generally, he attributes the memory lapse to the unconscious mind thinking of something else or remembering something else that then interferes with the thought process; the unconscious mind interrupting the conscious mind in order to interject something.

We need to figure out why our characters forget something. By investigating our characters and their stories we can get into their minds and understand the unconscious parts, explaining lapses of memory.

Elizabeth Loftus (1975) conducted several experiments examining the ability of people to recall events (memory). The experiments revolved around the common thought during her time, that eyewitnesses give reliable information. Looking at how the wording of a question influenced the recall of an event showed her how easy an investigator could influence a witness. An example of this would sound like "did you see the children getting on the school bus?" as opposed to, "did you see a school bus in the film?" Inserting the word "the" into the question, promotes more affirmative answers.

Memory does not play back like a recording like when we play a movie. Memories make up events that occur over time and when we recall them they intermix with not only the event that we recall, but any new information that we have taken in since that event. This causes the memory to be reconstructed based on the new information. By using the word "the" the questioner gives new information to the person recalling the event and that person reconstructs the event based on the new information. The person assumes that the questioner has the correct information about the event.

By understanding this, we as writers can play upon the retelling of events through our characters memory. We also must understand that when a character retells an event, the character will not necessarily give accurate information, but it will have some variance to what actually took place. Further, when the character recalls the event that took place in the middle of the night, the recalled event will most likely have inaccurate information intermixed with what really occurred. When creating our characters and exploring their growth during the story, their memories will affect this. The character may recall that his/her father molested him/her at night when in actuality the father just tucked the child in.

This concept of memory also ties nicely into dreams that our characters have. When we sleep we go through different stages. When we first fall asleep we enter stage 1 which is a light sleep, and progressively we move into deeper and deeper sleep (stage 4). We then cycle up until we approach stage 1 in which we enter a different kind of sleep called Rapid Eye Movement (REM). In this stage we begin to dream. We then go back and forth in between REM and Non-Rapid Eye Movement (NREM).

When we enter REM our bodies immobilize, which protects us from acting out our dreams. A study conducted by Dement showed that we need to dream. In fact, if a person goes without dreaming, the next night they will end up dreaming more than usual. The study also showed that when the researchers did not allow a participant to dream the participant gained a slight amount of weight.

As we write sleep into our characters' lives, we need to understand their sleep patterns and how they work. Do they get sleep or dream deprivation? They should have the "big" dreams in the morning when more people have dreams, or is this dream unique because it happens immediately upon falling asleep? Dreams can move our characters and give insight to our readers. Dreams also show flashbacks and foreshadowing.

How do dreams affect our characters? Do they believe in the dreams they have? After a character has a bad dream, do they remain grouchy for the rest of the day? Keep in mind the sleep patterns of our characters, and how sleeping on hard ground (if that's where they sleep) affects them.

IQ

Intelligence, better known as IQ, makes up another broad discussion topic by researchers. Can we narrow intelligence down to just one number or do we have multiple intelligences? Gardner, H. in 1983 proposed that we have multiple intelligences, which differed from the general historical belief. During the 20th century an individual's IQ was measured and referred to as "g". 'G' was basically a number that could be placed on a bell curve to show where individuals fell compared to other individuals. The higher the number the "smarter" the person and the better able that person supposedly functioned in life. This has changed today and 'G' gets used differently than in the past. During the 1970s and 1980s researchers began to question the idea that "G" told us everything about intelligence or IQ might actually include multiple intelligences, and in fact, researchers still highly debate this today.

In Gardner's theory, intelligence can't equate to just one number, several different areas get examined, which would have a different intelligence or number. Further, he explains that different parts of the brain take responsibility for different aspects of intelligence. Gardner came up with eight intelligences. Table 3 is a list of those intelligences and examples of a person who would fall into each one of those intelligences. Gardner surmised the idea that we may have a low score in one intelligence while high in another.

Table 3:

Multiple Intelligences

Intelligence	Examples of Individuals that score high in this intelligence
Linguistics	Shakespeare, J.K. Rowling, Dr. Seuss, Woody Allen
Musical	Mozart, Lauryn Hill, Andrea Boccelli, Paul McCartney
Logical-Mathematical	Albert Einstein, Carl Sagan, Marie Curie, B.F. Skinner
Spatial	Picasso, Frank Lloyd Wright, Leonardo DaVinci, Van Gogh
Bodily-kinesthetic	Charlie Chaplin, LeBron James, Serena and Venus Williams
Interpersonal	Ghandi, Abraham Maslow, Oprah Winfrey
Intrapersonal	Plato, Hermann Rorschach, Helen Keller, Bill Gates
Naturalist	Charles Darwin, Jane Goodall, Rachel Carson

Whether or not the theory is true is beside the point. When we create our characters, we need to look at their particular strengths and weaknesses. Often we forget that Heroes shine in certain areas, but they also have weaknesses. Maybe we create a character with extreme athletic ability but the character doesn't do a good job with introspection or a genius who needs support because he can barely move (i.e. Raistlan and Carman in the Dragonlance series). The more believable a character appears to the reader the more the reader will attach to that character.

Emotions

How do we create realistic emotions in our characters? When I revised my first book, my main character spent a lot of time crying. Every other scene he either cried or slept. It wears on the reader after a while. So let's talk about realistic emotions for our characters.

We need first to understand a little more about emotions and what they look like. Emotions are psychophysiological experiences in which bio-chemicals in our brain interact with external stimuli. A person's mood, temperament, personality, disposition and motivation influence the emotions of that individual. Many different theories exist about emotions and why or how they occur, but we will only look at one theory about emotions.

Joseph LeDoux (1996) postulated that we not only have emotional memories but that those emotional memories activate or convey quicker than cognitive memories. Evidence shows that we have different areas in our brains for cognitive memory and emotional memory. This means that when we start to experience a situation, if it parallels to past experiences, we remember the emotions behind that experience before we remember the exact details of the experience.

When we get into a stressful situation, we will react emotionally before cognitively. Although not always bad, many times it can spell disaster for us and the situation. For this reason, we get taught to take a deep breath before responding to stressful situations, to take time to think things through.

We writers easily get caught up with the cognitive reactions of our characters, because we think about what we write rather than feel. We need to remember that memories of past, highly emotional experiences fuel reactions. Those emotional memories will often cause the character to react on an emotional level rather than a cognitive one. We can use our characters' emotional reactions to set up problems. They see a person similar to their abusive father and they begin to cry, or they see a guy that reminds them of their loving father so they fall for the guy, who, in the end, turns out creepy.

When thinking about motivation, we need to ask the question "What does the person get from showing a particular emotion?" For example, why does a person cry when they are pulled over by a police officer? The person could truly be scared or only trying to manipulate the police officer into letting them off easy. By answering this question, we can understand our character better and how they function. It will also help us keep our characters consistent.

One person may react by crying, another by laughing, and another by anger to the exact same situation. This happens because of the differences in people's makeup. When we think about our character we need to figure out how and why they react the way they do.

With emotions comes romance. As writers we can use romance as a powerful tool to hook our readers. A study that looked at human sexuality, conducted by Masters and Johnson in the 60's, explored the fact that sex is as much or more a psychological experience as it is a biological one. Everyone gets a crush and falls in love. We can use romantic tension as one of the best ways to get a reader involved in our books. This being said, we need to try and avoid using clichés such as the romantic triangle that gets used over and over. We should look at all of the possible ways to use romance to build tension.

When creating our characters, we need to decide how much romance makes up their personality. Does the diehard romantic character gush over the roses or does the less romantic character just shrug at the roses? Keep in mind that men need romance just as much as women. How society looks at the romantic man and how it looks at the non-romantic woman will make a difference. To keep our characters consistent, we should consider how society will view that character when romance comes up. Also, as always, we need to think about the reasons. Remember the study by Harry Harlow and his monkeys.

When we talk about emotions we sometimes find ourselves putting two emotions on a continuum; by doing this we may not make the correct assumption about them. For example, love and hate. Do they lie on a continuum or are they just opposites? We generally think of love and hate as lying on a continuum and as you get closer to one you get farther from the other. This idea doesn't hold true. In fact, love and hate seem much closer than we think. A simple test of this is as follows: think about the people that we hurt the most in our lives. Generally speaking, the ones we tend to love the most we also hurt the most. This doesn't hold true for all people, of course.

This brings me to the importance of the relationship between the protagonist and the antagonist. These two concepts remain closely related, and play an important part in each other's realms. In the creation of our characters, what really happens within the lives of our characters and how they play off each other? Do they lay on a continuum or do they appear as opposites on the same end of the continuum, like love and hate.

The other emotions: sad, happy, anger, anxiety, shame, fear, guilt, surprise, friendship, wonder, kindness, we should also carefully consider and understand before using them in our stories.

The spirituality or non-spirituality of our characters influences their morals and belief systems. It impacts how they cope with things, both good and horrible. It impacts the way our characters react to situations, and make decisions. Spirituality and religion are two different things. When we create our characters, look at how spirituality and religion play a role in the character's life. Do they practice a religion, how does spirituality look for them, and what do they believe?

Think about our spirituality, our loved ones, our enemies, even the history of our world. The worlds that we create will have these components as well. Does the world you create worship many Gods? One God? How does the God in your world treat the people in the world? How does spirituality influence the worlds we create? How does our main character react to it? How do others react to our main character if he belongs to a certain religion?

Exercise: Make a list of emotions and how a character might 'show' that emotion. It's easy to 'tell' an emotion but much harder to show it. For example we could write: 'Molly was sad when her boyfriend left her that night.' Or we could really catch the attention of our reader by showing what Molly felt: 'Tears welled up in Molly's eyes and began to cascade down her face making a huge

pool at her feet as she watched her boyfriend walk away.'
Now I obviously exaggerated that sentence, but it sounds a
lot better than 'Molly was sad.'

Sample Characters

Looking at Gardners multiple intelligences Sarah
falls high in the interpersonal area and lower in the natural
area. She understands how others feel and can empathize
with them allowing her to build strong relationships with
others. This strength also helps her in leadership as she can
perceive how to navigate the nuances of differing opinions.
Her weakness in nature makes it difficult for her to
understand how nature plays a role in what happens to her
and the people she cares for. This weakness will influence
the decisions she makes and will be a way to show growth
through the story.

Emotions for Sarah lie close to the surface. This is a two edged sword for her. Because they are close to the edge, she has the ability to recognize when something in her world doesn't fit quite right. On the other hand, others can tell what she thinks about a certain situation or event, which they can use to manipulate her.

Ghiyath's strength also lies in his interpersonal intelligence. He has the ability to manipulate and control others through this ability giving him the ability to gain greater power. While interacting with others, Ghiyath can read their body language and react to that body language in an appropriate way to gain confidence, incite anger or fear. His weakness lies with his inability to understand self. He can't perceive the intrapersonal aspect of his life and for this reason he flounders.

Emotionally Ghiyath has learned to hide his pain and fears. He rarely shows an inappropriate emotional response to a situation. This has helped him gain the trust of others and allows him to show an inner confidence that doesn't really exist.

Chapter 10
Change and Motivation

If we can change, then things may continue to get better. One of the drawbacks, of course, things may get worse. We all go through change in many different areas. We all started out as one cell and have grown into adults. We have grown more mature and hopefully, have learned to control our emotions and our behaviors. We have also grown in what we know and how to apply that knowledge. Our societies, environments and technologies have also changed around us. We learn to adapt and mold to the environments that we live in and move to. We have learned to adapt through times of war and peace, prosperity and poverty. We need to understand how we and those around us have changed in various situations. This will help us develop our characters and plan where we want them to end up. This chapter will look at those things that change to some degree or another as well as some of the things that don't appear to change. We will begin by talking about personality; a part of us that many psychologists believe can't change.

When we try to figure out why a person does something, we make an error called the "fundamental attribution error." Think about someone cutting you off in traffic. How do you describe that person? What thoughts come to mind? Studies have found that generally we overweigh attributes that remain stable, things that don't change (race, age, sex and personality) and under weigh attributes that do change (pregnant wife in the car, texting on cell phone, sick).

Personality doesn't change and yet, how often do we try to change our own personality or someone else's. Lord of The Rings has many different types of change. Study the difference between how Frodo, Sam, Pippin, and

Merry change. Their personality, race, and gender all stay the same, yet their behaviors change. At the end, Pippin and Merry still goof off, but they're more responsible. Sam remains the mother hen, but he has a lot more confidence. Frodo persists, but has a much greater weight on him. Their behaviors and the way they look at the world change, but their personalities stay the same.

People change subtly. Look at the people we have known the longest. How do they change? Have you noticed the changes? Our characters need to change in increments, barely perceptible by the reader. They can change over time, except in extreme instances, but their personalities will remain the same. At the end of a story readers should recognize that change has occurred in the characters or how the characters did not change, but while reading, it should seem almost imperceptible. Frodo changed in slow and steady ways.

Behavior can and does change in us and in our characters as well. Looking at the ABC's (Antecedent, Behavior, and Consequence) of behaviorism, we can see that we can't really change the antecedent, but we can change our behavior, which changes the consequence. When working with clients, clinicians will look at the antecedents and the behavior that follows, and explain the consequence of that behavior. Clinicians then look at what would result from different behaviors. This will hopefully help the client see that a different behavior brings about better consequences, and then change occurs. When a client sees that changing a behavior to an antecedent changes the consequence for the better, they show more willingness to change that behavior.

Perspective can also change. I use guided imagery to help people see past experiences, then work with them to see those experiences through "healthy adult" eyes. By understanding past experiences through the healthy adult perspective, they can then understand why things happened. For example, the kid who runs toward the street hears his mom yelling at him. He thinks mom is mad… I'm a bad person… You can see where this can go. When we take them through guided imagery the healthy adult sees the scene from the mother's perspective, she fears that her child could get hit by a car and die. The healthy adult no longer thinks that he was a bad child and mother was mad, only that mother feared for him and tried to get his attention so that he didn't get hurt.

The perspective of our characters will change as they experience new things. They may have a conversation with a person from a different nation and learn their perspective on a war. This will change the character's perspective on the situation.

Emotions about a situation can change as well. A clinician could explore this through guided imagery as well. The clinician helps the client see how and where these feelings come from. The clinician helps the client see the situation through a "healthy adult's" eyes to get a better perspective of the situation, this then enables the client to handle the emotions that correspond to the event. By changing the emotional memory of a situation, we can then help the person change the behavior of similar events. As writers we show our readers how our characters see things differently and react differently to similar events, circumstances and people. Keep in mind that most of our characters don't have clinicians there by their side. So, who is helping your character? Or does your character gain some knowledge/self-awareness that helps that character change that emotion?

Irrational thoughts change. Cognitive behaviorists employ many different tools to help modify irrational thoughts. One tool the therapist might employ to help the client is to have the client confront and challenge the irrational thoughts. They scrutinize with a different perspective. Once again we show our reader the change in thought process of our characters through the characters change in behavior.

If we want to show our readers that our characters have changed, we need to put the characters in similar situations throughout our novels. By doing this we establish in the beginning how our characters normally behave and then show, through the course of the book, in similar situations, how the characters change their behaviors and reactions.

We, as writers, must set up situations that will change the behavior, thoughts, emotions, perspective, and feelings of our characters. The letter found, the loved one who dies, the sermon that touches the heart, the challenges that bend but don't break the character, and the unconditional personal regard from a person whom the character respects.

This leads us into the next highly debatable question of, "Why do people change?" To know our characters better we need to ask, "Why do our characters change?" There exist quite a few theories out there on why we change and as long as you keep it consistent it doesn't matter really what theory you employ. I personally feel that when it takes more energy to stay how we are than it does to change, we change.

When people don't realize the amount of energy they use to stay the same, it can be difficult to change. Think about those who stay in their addictions. They use extreme amounts of energy to stay in the same state. They have to worry about going to jail, their next fix, their loved ones no longer wanting to include them, and on and on, yet they stay the same. It seems that the individual would see that to give up the drugs and addiction would make things much easier, and use less energy, but often they don't. James O. Prochaska explained that the realization that change must happen occurs second in the process of change.

Prochaska, in 1977, developed the Transtheoretical model of change. This model includes five stages of change that a person goes through. The first stage called **pre-contemplation** the person doesn't want to make the change and really doesn't realize that they need to change. In the second stage, **Contemplation**, a person begins to weigh the costs and benefits of change. The person still doesn't change but starts to see that change must happen. The third stage, called the **preparation** stage, the individual has finally decided that change must occur, and that they will do something. **Action,** the fourth stage, a person actually changes and does something different. The final stage, **maintenance** stage, the individual has changed and learns to maintain the change.

Remember, that people resist change and that includes our characters. They need something that will push them to the point that it takes more energy to stay the same than it does to change. We, as writers, must understand our characters limits, their breaking points that send them too far and the point that pushes them to change.

When we have high amounts of stress for sustained periods our body is telling us something needs to change. On the other hand, low levels of stress actually get the body prepared for fight or flight, not necessarily change. A study conducted by Holmes and Rahe in 1967 investigated how to measure life stresses and what makes up life stresses.

They sent out a survey with 43 life events, marriage being a reference point having a score of 50 points. The respondents would then rate the life stresses dependent on this point either marking them higher or lower.

The top ten events included death of spouse, divorce, marital separation, jail term, death of close family member, personal injury or illness, marriage, fired at work, marital reconciliation, and retirement. The bottom ten comprised of: minor violations of the law, Christmas, vacation, change in eating habits, change in frequency of family gatherings, change in sleeping habits, small mortgage, change in social activities, change in church activities, and change in recreation.

The researchers point out that in each situation it required change, adaptation or coping on the part of the person. Even a positive event may still cause stress. The researchers went on to show that this stress directly relates to illness and hopelessness.

This leads into how we look at the stress of our characters. How do the changes in their lives stress them? How do they cope with it? Make a list of the stressors our characters experience and then calculate that stress. If it appears high, make sure the story shows this and how that character deals with that stress.

How people perceive their ability to change plays an important factor of change. Julian Rotter, in 1966, designed a scale to evaluate the degree of control people believe they have over their fate and called the scale the I-E Scale, I for internal and E for external. The closer the individual associates to the 'I,' the more they felt in control over their fate. The closer an individual connects to 'E,' the more they felt they had little control of their fate.

Further, "I" people bet on sure things, whereas "E" people take risks. "I" people influence the attitudes of others more than others influencing them; however, the opposite is true for "E" people. Three things that Rotter reported as possible reasons people become an 'I' or an 'E' individual: socioeconomic status, upbringing, and culture. In general, if our character approaches the 'I' person, there must be some reason for it. Additionally, characters will believe a certain way if they feel in control. That belief can change in either direction. For example, a character born in an alley gets rescued by a loving family who takes care of his/her needs. In the beginning, the character may believe that fate played a role in his/her rescue from the alley, but later believes that due to his/her greater diligence than the other children born in the alley he/she pulled him/herself out of the alley.

Peoples' ability to change increases as their power and control increases. We add to this idea by saying that the more power and control a person has, the more change they can make, relieving stress and discomfort which leads to better health and happiness. Langer and Rodin, in 1976, proved this in a study at a rest home by giving half of the participants increased-responsibility in their treatment while the others continued with their normal routine. The results of the study showed that by giving participants more responsibility, their health and happiness increased. On a follow up study 18 months later, the researchers found another significant occurrence. 30% of participants not involved in the treatment died, while in the group receiving treatment only 15% died. Keep in mind that the demographics and characteristics of the groups remained the same. Personal power and control over one's life factors greatly impact how happy and productive an individual feels.

Another study stated the idea that having too many choices decreases happiness. In 2000, Iyengar and Lepper conducted a study in which participants had the option to buy jams and chocolates and to do an extra credit essay. One group of the participants received 6 choices while the other group had 24 or 30 choices. The results showed that when participants received fewer choices, a significant more amount of participants would buy the chocolate and write the essay than those given more choices. Also, those who had fewer choices showed greater satisfaction with their choices.

Our stories will present our characters with many different choices and decisions to make. They can choose to accept the quest or not. However, to write into our stories more choices for our characters, more ways to slay the dragon or to not slay the dragon at all will make the story even more interesting. Show characters having the ability to choose and how they take responsibility for their choices and also how characters react with too many choices. How do our characters behave coming out of orphanages (or a number of other confining institutions) and into a new world of responsibilities and decisions?

One influential study by Kahneman and Tversky in 1979 examined why people make risky decisions. They found that people make decisions based on losses and gains as opposed to the probability of those losses or gains. "Imagine your country is preparing for the outbreak of a disease expected to kill 600 people. If program A is adopted, exactly 200 people will be saved. If program B is adopted there is a 33% chance that 600 people will be saved and a 66% chance that zero people will be saved." In this example, more people chose option A (72%) because the example was presented in gains.

"Imagine your country is preparing for the outbreak of a disease expected to kill 600 people. If program A is adopted, exactly 400 people will die. If program B is adopted there is a 1/3 probability that no one will die and 2/3 probability that 600 people will die." Because the researchers presented option B as a loss more participants chose it (78%). From this example we learn that people don't care about the odds of something happening, but they worry more about loss.

When writing our stories we need to watch our ultimatums. Do we write them from the perspective of odds or from gains and losses? Characters will more likely make the choice depending on the loss. Take for example the case of Frodo in *The Lord of The Rings* series. When Frodo heard about the ring and the destruction it would bring, he didn't care until he realized that same destruction would include the shire. His decision came from the fear of losing the shire, not on the odds of success. Characters change when they see a choice as a loss rather than odds. By increasing the gains and losses our characters feel will force them to act.

A character can also determine change through self-fulfilling prophecy. Rosenthal and Jacobson in 1966 found that expectations of teachers influenced gains by students. Specifically, the researchers identified several students as bright students to their teachers; when in actuality the researchers had randomly assigned the students with nothing specifically special about them. By the end of the year the test score of the identified students in younger grades (1st-4th) gained as much as 30 points on the test while the control group, those not specified to teachers as being bright, gained around 12 points. The experimenters found that when a teacher expects a student to do well, they will do much better than if the teacher expects them to do poorly. Since Rosenthal and Jacobson many other researchers have replicated this study and the findings still hold true today.

Another interesting story about a horse called, "Clever Hans" further illustrates the idea of self-fulfilling prophecy. This horse could read and write and do simple math. After studying further, investigators found that the experimenters conducting the tests to see if Clever Hans could do math, read, and write gave subtle hints to the horse. The first hint came after they asked the question; they would look at the horses hoof for an answer, queuing the horse to start stomping his hoof. Second, when the horse approached the correct response they would look up slightly, once again queuing the horse. The horse read the subtle movements and "expectations" of the experimenters, not actually able to read or do math.

Think about the stories we read and the movies we watch. The main characters almost always have someone who believes in him/her. That person expects the main character to succeed. Who expects your main character to succeed? How does your main character react to those expectations? And most importantly, who believes in and supports you? How do you live up to those expectations and self-fulfilling prophecies?

A final note on motivation and change revolves around the idea of regret. Just as we have regrets, our characters will have regrets. Think about our "perfect" main characters who always do the right things without any regrets. To make our characters alive and real for our readers, we need to give them regrets – both selfish and selfless. Meaning the character should regret yelling at his mom, or regret not kissing his best friends girlfriend.

Exercise: Take an afternoon looking back at the times you have changed. What caused those changes? What inspired you to change for the better? Keep in mind the times you changed for the worse? What happened in those moments? By doing this you will learn about what motivates you. Next apply this knowledge to a character, putting that character into similar situations to create change.

Sample Characters

Love of family and society motivate Sarah to change. She sees that by changing herself she can change the situations of others. In the beginning of her story, she loses everything and sinks into despair, feeling all is lost.

When she begins to see that others can make up her family, she changes from despair to hope.

Others see power as motivating Ghiyath and Ghiyath would agree with this, but looking on the inside, one can see that the true motivation for Ghiyath is belonging. Ghiyath wants to feel that he belongs and that others need and care about him, but he can't reach this due to his inability to let go of the past and the pain that he holds inside him. For this reason his story doesn't revolve around change but the lack of change and the sadness this creates for him.

Conclusion

As we continue to study the concepts and practice the strategies that we have learned in this book our characters will come alive. They will look more and more like the people we interact with every day. In the end our characters become real, just as Pinocchio became a real boy.

www.ingramcontent.com/pod-product-compliance
Lightning Source LLC
Chambersburg PA
CBHW070642290526
45790CB00001B/164